Forgiving Yourself

Forgiving Yourself

A Step-by-Step Guide to Making Peace with Your Mistakes and Getting On with Your Life

Beverly Flanigan, M.S.S.W.

Book design by Anne Scatto/PIXEL PRESS

Library of Congress Cataloging-in-Publication data
Flanigan, Beverly.
Forgiving yourself: a step-by-step guide to making peace with your
mistakes and getting on with your life / by Beverly Flanigan.
          p.   cm.
Includes bibliographical references and index.
ISBN 0-02-538682-4
    1. Forgiveness.   2. Self-evaluation.   3. Peace of mind.
I. Title
BF637.F67F535   1996   96-1106
158'.1—dc20   CIP

10 9 8 7 6 5 4 3 2 1

Contents

Foreword

I began my examination of forgiveness in 1980 as part of my work as a fellow of the Kellogg Foundation. Since that time, I have lectured on, written about, and counseled people who have been successful in forgiving themselves and others.

My first book, *Forgiving the Unforgivable* (Macmillan Publishing, 1992), describes a six-phase process that people can employ to forgive others who injure them. Information for the book was gathered from interviews with people who had been successful in forgiving children's murderers, spouses who abandoned them, parents who abused them, and a profound and frightening plethora of injuries perpetrated by loved ones.

Information for *Forgiving Yourself* was gathered from some of the same people who described the concurrent process of self-forgiveness they engaged in as they struggled to forgive those who injured them. In addition, data were gathered from two other sources. During my workshops on forgiving others, I asked people who had faced the task of forgiving themselves to complete a four-page questionnaire on self-forgiveness. Questions elicited information about people's age, educational background, family constellation, religious affiliation, and specific descriptions of the situations people forgave themselves for, including the process they used. These questionnaires were also distributed by professional colleagues and personal acquaintances who gave them to their work associates, church groups, and friends for completion. The data, then, are not scientifically gathered, but do reflect the experiences of approximately 110 people. Moreover, some materials presented in the following pages are drawn from clinical experiences of my own, or my students', clientele. Names have been changed throughout the book to ensure anonymity. I am grateful to all who shared their stories. Case examples I have developed for teaching purposes are also used. Statements in quotation marks are direct quotes from interviewed persons or questionnaire participants.

Self-forgiveness may be at the very core of peacemaking. When people forgive others, they stop hatred in its track and refuse to allow it to pour onto others. When people forgive themselves, they also stop hatred in its track and refuse to allow self-loathing to dominate their lives and to spill over onto their children, spouses, friends, and neighbors. A person's self-loathing can be every bit as lethal to others as hatred in any other form. Hatred poisons, no matter to whom it is directed.

It is my hope that *Forgiving Yourself* will provide damaged people the tools to put self-hatred away and return to the human community. If the book serves this purpose, then another source of information about individual healing will have an impact on something even more important than personal well-being: it will also serve to play some small part in healing us all.

I would like to thank my agent and all the friends, coworkers, and editors who supported and helped me through the process of writing this book. I would like to give special thanks to the people who cared enough about other people to respond to my call for interviews and to talk with me about their experiences.

Introduction

What Is Self-Forgiveness?

If you selected *Forgiving Yourself* from a bookshelf, you are probably a person who knows too well the pain of recognizing that something you did or are has damaged your life and the lives of others. The damage may be to your close relationships, to people you barely know, to your spiritual relationship with a higher power, or to your relationship with yourself. If your words or actions have driven loved ones away; if blindness to your limitations has resulted in hurting someone else; or if your reluctance to see yourself realistically has resulted in a rupture with what you have assumed about yourself, then you are poised to begin the process of forgiving yourself.

What is self-forgiveness? How does it happen? Is self-forgiveness just accepting yourself? Is self-forgiveness arrogant or dangerous? Some would answer that others must forgive us or that God must forgive us before we can forgive ourselves. Self-forgiveness can restore peace within a person, and when peace is restored and hatred eliminated—even self-hatred—good things can result. Self-forgiveness is a process that can coexist when others forgive us for hurting them, or when God is at work. But being forgiven by another does not preempt the need for self-forgiveness.

Self-forgiveness is a specific process that results in several outcomes. First, self-forgiveness results in your being able to finally feel that you have paid your debt to those you think you have owed. Second, self-forgiveness ends the desire to continue punishing yourself for letting your flaws or mistakes hurt other people. Third, self-forgiveness requires a commitment to personal change, and once you change, you will feel better about yourself. Finally, when you have forgiven yourself, the things you have believed about yourself and other people begin to make sense again. Your ideas about life are no longer troubling or incongruent. Your life and its meaning seem to fit again into the "big picture."

The process of forgiving yourself is not easy. Self-forgiveness results from an honest, sometimes very painful, confrontation with ourselves that being forgiven by another person does not require. Other people may forgive us, but they may not know us as well as we know ourselves. Only we can know how mean or arrogant or blind to our limitations we have been. It is this knowledge that makes self-forgiveness so hard, maybe harder than forgiving another.

What Self-Forgiveness Is and Is Not

Self-forgiveness always has to do with relationships. Forgiveness of oneself is called for when relationships have been permanently altered because of our actions, inactions, words, and some might argue, even thoughts. Self-forgiveness does not apply to aspects of yourself that have hurt you, and you alone. For example, a person does not need to forgive herself when she has gained too much weight to fit into a favorite dress or when she has failed a test as a result of not studying hard enough. She may regret these situations and be faced with accepting her flaws, but self-acceptance is not at all the same as self-forgiveness. Each requires a very different healing process. Self-acceptance focuses on oneself and discovering or creating a better self-concept. Self-forgiveness focuses on other people and allows us to transform ourselves into better people for the sake of others. Self-forgiveness does not result in the conclusion, "I'm okay; you're okay." On the contrary, self-forgiveness requires a person to acknowledge that something about herself has not been okay, and, in fact, has damaged important parts of one's life and the lives of others. Self-forgiveness is the process of self-examination that results in the conclusion, "I must change. I'm not okay." Who benefits from self-forgiveness? Isn't self-forgiveness a dangerous and even cynical way for a person to let herself off the moral hook and give her license to offend other people again? No. People who suffer after they have harmed their relationships are not able to let themselves off, morally. Instead, they are burdened down with guilt or regret for what they have done. A person brave enough to confront her flaws is a potential asset to others, not a danger. One who is blind to the parts of herself that can wound others is dangerous.

PEOPLE WHO SEEK SELF-FORGIVENESS

People who seek to forgive themselves are people of conscience. People who lack conscience, by contrast, have no concept of the pain they may cause others, or may feel no particular concern even if they know they have harmed other people. Sociopaths and psychopaths feel no need to forgive themselves; they are unconcerned about the pain they may cause. People who struggle to forgive themselves for the mistakes they make are, by contrast, people with ordinary or even extraordinary consciences and well-developed senses of right and wrong. We can easily see the difference between the mugger of an old woman sneering at the court cameras and the shriveled, guilty-looking man who, in hunger, broke into a house to steal money. For the first person, non-forgiveness is not an issue. Having little conscience and therefore little empathy for his victim or remorse for his violence, he will see no need to forgive himself. By contrast, the second man, believing he is wrong, will have to live with the guilt of his conscience perhaps for the rest of his life. Self-forgiveness occurs in people who are aware of their impact on others. For this reason, our families and our society need people to be able to forgive themselves.

It is also important, however, for people to understand when they have done nothing that merits forgiveness. Others in their lives may attempt to persuade them that they have been wrong or bad in some way, and that they should experience shame and guilt. People who feel bad about themselves—that is, who experience subjective feelings of having hurt someone—can achieve self-forgiveness; but there must also be objective verification from outside someone that self-forgiveness is required or even appropriate.

Many people are clever at drawing others into a sense of obligation or shame. Perceived obligations can make people feel bad when objectively they should not. If you want to attempt to forgive yourself, you must first undertake a careful, critical assessment of yourself and your situation to discern whether there is really something to feel bad about or whether others are manipulating your emotions. This process will be discussed in detail later.

CONDITIONS THAT REQUIRE SELF-FORGIVENESS

What conditions require self-forgiveness as opposed to self-acceptance? Aside from the first condition, that self-forgiveness is needed when we have hurt others, there are five additional characteristic situations that indicate a person needs to learn self-forgiveness. These conditions are as follows:

1. Causing injuries that result from mistakes, wrongdoings, or limitations
2. Causing harm that challenges or alters our central personal sets of assumptions
3. When apologies from others do not seem to correct the situation
4. When an injurer is exposed to her "self-as-feared"*[1]
5. One or more of four these discrete emotions are felt by the person who must forgive herself: guilt, shame, regret, or grief

---

*The "self-as-feared" is what a person privately worries that she may be. One person may worry that she is, at the core, evil or cruel. Another wonders if he is unstable or oversexed. Others privately fear that they may be pathological liars or "fakes." The "self-as-feared" is a secret, unexposed.

MISTAKES

A *mistake* is defined as "a harmful, rash, impulsive or foolish act"[2] or "an error in action, opinion, or judgment."[3] Mistakes can be made through action or inaction, omission or commission. For example, one person looks into her empty wallet after just losing her entire week's wages in a slot machine. She has made a mistake of commission. She behaved in an impulsive way and made an error in judgment. Another person decides not to put her week's wages on a winning horse that paid 25 to 1. Her mistake was one of omission, which is also an error in judgment.

A mistake is always neutral morally. Mistakes are neither good nor bad when considered independent of their results. Mistakes take on moral properties only in their results and become hard to forgive when they cause something bad to happen. Let's say that a person goes out to chop down a dead tree and does not check for the presence of people nearby. When the tree crushes picnickers in a neighboring meadow, the neutral act of cutting the tree becomes an error in judgment that causes great harm. The tree cutter may be unable to forgive himself.

When morally neutral action is not taken and great harm results, a state of non-forgiveness can erupt. A woman who did not tell her teenage son about the dangers of unprotected sex blames herself for his contracting HIV. Her "act of omission," she thinks, destroyed his life. For this she cannot forgive herself.

Mistakes are errors; mistakes that require forgiveness are errors that result in harm or do not produce good when good was possible. A mistake might be a person's not having intervened or not having said a kind word; or it might result from taking a certain action at just the wrong time.

Forgiving your mistakes, though, is different from forgiving your transgressions. Transgressions are the second source of unforgiven injuries.

TRANSGRESSIONS

Transgressions are actions taken that pass over or go beyond certain moral limits. To transgress means, literally, to "go across," as to go across a boundary or barrier. Transgressions that cause people's inability to forgive themselves have certain properties that are similar to mistakes. But there are key differences.

A transgression, unlike a mistake, is not morally neutral. It is wrong, regardless of whether it alters any relationship or is even detected by another. A person who lusts after her neighbor's husband may feel guilty of her transgression even if she never acts upon her thoughts. She might find herself unable to forgive herself for her thoughts if she belongs to a religion that emphasizes the wrongness of (and need for repentance for) such things. "Worse than mistakes, transgressions are forbidden, illegal, immoral, or questionably moral acts."[4]

Transgressions can cross over a variety of moral boundaries—codes such as the Ten Commandments, laws established by society, or personal commitments made by individuals. Sam violated a legal boundary and a personal one at the same time.

Sam, forty-four at the time he wrote, still had trouble forgiving himself for something he did when he was twenty: He caused a car accident. The other driver was a pregnant woman. He was required, by law, to repair the woman's car, but for more than a month he did nothing. For this, he was given a warning by the insurance company; still he did nothing. He writes:

> *"I was at a self-centered stage in my life and didn't care that I had caused an accident; and then I was irresponsible in making amends. . . . I did not fix the car with proper materials, and even put off fixing it for over a month while she was incapacitated.*
>
> *"I was only embarrassed at the time because I got the warning; but later on I found it hard to forgive myself. . . ."*

Sam had trouble forgiving himself, not so much because he broke a law, but because he violated his own sense of personal morality. Personal ideas of right and wrong are unique to each individual. Laws and civil codes, by contrast, protect individuals from each other when there is disagreement about what is right or wrong. Legal transgressions are quite separate from moral transgressions.

LEGAL TRANSGRESSIONS

Legal transgressions might include stealing, civil disobedience, assault and battery, diverting money into shady business dealings, or improperly recycling your trash. In other words, the violation of a city code or a state or federal statute is a legal transgression. Society sets forth rules that we are all expected to abide by, regardless of whether we agree with them. People who transgress legal codes or laws may or may not have trouble forgiving themselves depending on how strongly they agree with the laws they violated.

Legal transgressions are violations of one kind of rule only—legal rules. Moral transgressions can be violations of two kinds of rules, interpersonal agreements about right and wrong or religious moral codes.

MORAL TRANSGRESSIONS

Moral transgressions between people are special kinds of wrongdoings. They are special because when two people form a relationship, their separate ideas of right and wrong combine to form a new construct of right and wrong, unique to those two people. The new construct reflects people's religious beliefs, education, gender, and even their ages. For example, two older people, raised before the Great Depression, might share an opinion that to ask each other a very personal question would be intrusive or morally wrong. Two teenagers in the 90s, by contrast, are likely to see nothing wrong with inquiring about each other's family, sexuality, or religion—all once considered taboo. When people transgress moral agreements with friends or spouses, colleagues or employers, they cross the barriers of their own ideas about right and wrong by lying, withholding information, taking resources, or withholding truth to have more of something (perhaps more money, more sex, or more objects) or less of something (less need to justify their opinions or decisions).

Moral rules, in addition to being part of people's interpersonal relationships, are also set down in religious scripture; and they are violated for the same reasons that interpersonal rules are: Religious rules are violated by people who expect the violations to profit them. The teachings found in the New Testament, the Talmud, Buddhist scriptures, and most of the major world religions provide specific delineations of what constitutes right or wrong thoughts and actions. If people steal, lie, murder, commit adultery, or are envious or jealous of others, they are likely to have violated religious codes of right and wrong. Transgressions may hurt people who are betrayed, but they may also hurt the betrayer's relationship with God because violated religious covenants are spiritual betrayals.

Transgressions are committed with selfish purposes in mind. They are not morally neutral, like mistakes. A person must take responsibility for a transgression to achieve self-forgiveness. When people engage in transgressions, they know what they are doing. There is intent involved in transgressions where there is no intent in a mistake. If you have violated a moral code with another person or a written code that has guided your spiritual life, you may have trouble forgiving yourself because you intended the wrongdoing. You chose to engage in selfish and wrong behavior knowing that you might damage your relationships. Still, self-forgiveness is possible with hard work and personal change.

TRANSGRESSIONS WITH EVIL INTENT

A transgression is committed by someone to gain personal advantage. A teenager lies to her parents about chaperons being at a party because she knows if she tells them the truth, they won't let her go. You may lie about being unable to come to the phone because you would rather continue to watch TV. These transgressions, though, are not likely to evoke the need for forgiveness. They have no malice in their intent. They are rooted, maybe, in self-service but not in malice. Even if a fire broke out at the unchaperoned party and the teenager sustained massive burns, she might have trouble forgiving herself for lying and damaging the trust of her parents, but she does not have to forgive herself for evil in her heart.

Transgressions with evil intent share the same properties as other transgressions. They have an inherent moral wrongness and violate a moral boundary for personal advantage. But they differ in one key way: in evil transgressions, a transgressor intends to injure others.

Transgressions with evil intent might include abusing a child, blowing up a building with people inside, acting in a specific way that is designed to lead a person into injury, or any number of actions taken or words spoken with the intent of harming others. Murders, child abusers, and batterers engage in evil transgressions.

Mistakes, transgressions, and evil transgressions gain moral gravity and greater weight on a scale similar to legal ideas of misdemeanors and felonies. Mistakes that cause harm are generally *misdemeanors*. *Felonies* where there is no intent (like drunk driving that results in a death) are less grave, morally at least, than felonies with intent (like first-degree murder); but people may be unable to forgive themselves for any one of the three.

The pain of non-forgiveness is rooted in your mistakes, transgressions, evil transgressions, or the fourth source—your own shortcomings and limitations. When beginning the process of self-forgiveness, it will be imperative for you to accurately identify which of the four sources of non-forgiveness you must reconcile.

SHORTCOMINGS AND LIMITATIONS

A *shortcoming* is "the condition or fact of failing to reach an expected or required standard of character or performance."[5] A *limitation* is a less inclusive idea, meaning "a restrictive weakness or lack of capacity."[6] Both ideas relate to personal characteristics. Both may be acquired or innate. Either can result in damage to the self or another person so grave that it can be considered unforgivable.

Innate shortcomings and limitations might be physical or mental. For example, a person may be brighter or less bright than someone else, taller or less tall, stronger or less strong. A limitation can appear to be an attribute until it causes harm. The very bright professor who cannot understand her daughter's school difficulties and places such demands for performance on the girl that the daughter runs away may be as unable to forgive herself as the mother whose low IQ prevents her from recognizing that her child's high fever will cause the child permanent deafness. Both will have trouble forgiving themselves because their limitations harmed their children.

Shortcomings may lead a person into committing a mistake. They are neutral morally. They may be regrettable; but taken alone, they are neutral. Cowardice and fear of the dark, heights, or water are neutral until a person cannot help her friend who is lost in the dark or stuck on a cliff or drowning in a river. The exposure of such shortcomings may give rise to the need for self-forgiveness. Acquired shortcomings may bother people more than innate ones because they are more readily recognized and modified. A talented equestrienne takes a bad fall from her horse and lets her fear of riding dominate her. Because she can ride well, she might be more likely to have trouble forgiving herself for not intervening if a runaway horse with a disabled child plunged over a cliff than the non-rider nearby who was also afraid to attempt the rescue. The latter has to forgive herself for cowardice—the former for allowing circumstances to destroy her capacity to act and assist another human being. When people's shortcomings are hidden deep in the psyche and are only recognized when they finally result in injury to others, then the pain of remaining unforgiven can consume a person until the process of self-forgiveness begins.

Changing Our Life Assumptions

When a person so damages a relationship that she cannot forgive herself, she may find that some of the central assumptions she has about herself need to be looked at and changed. We all have assumptions about who we are that make it possible to live our lives with minimal fear or chaos. These assumptions are called by one author "the bedrock of our conceptual system. . . . "[7] People have, I suggest, at least six essential assumptions about their lives: 1) the world is benevolent; 2) the world is meaningful; 3) the self is worthy;[8] 4) the world is, to some degree, predictable; 5) people have some control over matters in their personal lives; 6) a principle of justice is at work in the world.[9] In other words, people generally believe that their lives and the people and circumstances in them are good, somewhat predictable, and in their control. But researchers are beginning to see that these assumptions can be shattered by natural disasters such as floods, tornadoes, hurricanes, and windstorms; by other human beings; by events such as crimes and wars; and by oneself when she has injured those in her life.

Traumas come in many forms: natural, those caused by others, and unfortunately, those brought on by ourselves. The trauma of being unable to forgive ourselves is brought on by our own mistakes, wrongdoings, and personal limitations. Like other traumas, they permanently damage our bedrock assumptions that we are inherently good or that our worlds are orderly. When we ruin our own relationships, we assault the assumption that the world is benevolent. When a person cannot forgive herself, it is precisely for the damage she has done to her own worldview. You have probably been faced with the erosion of your self-esteem, the loss of faith in your belief that the world is a good place, or that you will always have a special place in it. You may also wonder if God still cares for you when you have been responsible for hurting others or yourself.

Sam, who did not repair the damaged car, learned at twenty that self-worth is not a "given." It must be earned. The same is true if you cannot forgive yourself. The assumptive set that held your world together is gone and must be replaced with other meanings and other assumptions if self-forgiveness is to occur. Rebuilding meaning is a key task of the self-forgiveness process.

UNFORGIVEN INJURIES AND APOLOGIES

Most people who are unable to forgive themselves know all too well that an apology does not bring about self-forgiveness. An apology begins an interpersonal process of forgiveness that is finalized when the offended person takes the offending party back into her life, and both parties once again agree to the moral terms of their relationship.[10]

People who are unable to forgive themselves most likely have one of three experiences with an apology: They apologize, but the apology is not accepted; they apologize and the apology is accepted, but the damage done to one's self-worth is too great to be affected by the apology; or there is no one to apologize to. A soldier may be unable to forgive himself for the brutality he inflicted on women and children in Vietnam. Three of the soldier's critical assumptions about himself as worthy and the world as both meaningful and benevolent are totally shattered. The soldier cannot bring back those he killed by apologizing nor can he free himself of his guilt by attempting to apologize to himself. He needs to engage in the much more complex and rigorous process of self-forgiveness.

An apology does not result in either another's forgiveness or self-forgiveness. It may put forgiveness into motion, but an apology, alone, cannot effect full forgiveness. When people cannot forgive themselves, the true nature of personal impotence is learned. Your actions have changed someone else's world, your world, and your belief in yourself, but you can do nothing with an apology to restore a sense of self-worth, reestablish old assumptions, or repair relationships. An apology alone has no power to do these things. Words of apology may comfort and appease people, but they are not enough to mend broken beliefs.

UNFORGIVEN INJURIES REVEAL THE "SELF-AS-FEARED"

Most people believe that they are "good," even above average.[11] Research shows that most people think highly of themselves. They take pride in their successes and are likely to feel that something outside themselves is responsible for their failures. But many people, too, fear that underneath their successes and public (or even private) personae, lurks a less-than-average or even essentially false person. A person may glimpse her "self-as-feared" during a temper tantrum or while delivering a verbal assault to a spouse or child. The "self-as-feared" can make itself known in one's private thoughts, possibly thoughts of greed, cruelty, or violence. Some of us have had the experience of having previously hidden parts of ourselves suddenly made public. A popular and "sweet" high school girl is observed by a large number of other students screaming nastily at her partially blind grandmother at a shopping mall.

Moments that reveal an underlying part of ourselves might occur when only we become aware of our "darker parts"—for example, when a usually calm mother in the anger of a moment raises a hand to her youngster and is shocked at herself. Or those moments might reveal to us and another at the same time a previously hidden aspect of our nature— a limitation or shortcoming.

When these incidents happen, the person sees a side of herself that, unless she is able to immediately deny the incident or shift responsibility to another, reveals a capacity toward meanness or nastiness. Or incidents like these may put an ignored limitation into sharp focus. Limitations, mistakes, or transgressions that alter relationships and shatter assumptions reveal hidden sides of people. There is exposure; and it cannot be contained.

Each person probably carries a petty trait of some sort. Some of us are lucky enough to have no one see it. Some of us let it emerge, but we are not punished or shamed by it. People who cannot forgive themselves aren't so lucky. They live with their darker, weaker sides exposed. They are unable to use common psychological defense mechanisms, such as denial or intellectualization, to shield themselves from the unwanted recognition that the harm they caused is real and permanent.

A person who sees his unsavory characteristics can ignore them or attempt to reconcile himself to his weaknesses. A person who decides to try to forgive himself reconciles himself to his weaknesses and vows to change.

GUILT, SHAME, REGRET, AND GRIEF

Guilt, shame, regret, and grief are closely linked, but they are not the same emotion. Entire books have been written that describe and discuss regret, shame, and grief,[12] and there are numerous treatises on guilt.[13] Simple distinctions among these feelings, however, can be made. *Guilt* is a person's subjective experience of feeling bad for having transgressed.[14] It is linked to doing something wrong, and so is a moral notion. It is also one of the "guardian emotions"—that is, guilt causes people discomfort, but the discomfort guards against one person's decision to commit a wrongdoing against another. The anticipation of guilt can keep people from harming each other.

Shame is the subjective experience of feeling bad about oneself, but not for having transgressed. A person experiences shame when he *is* something, and when what he is has been exposed for others to see.[15] People feel shame when they are compared to others, but fall short in the comparison. Shame is said to be a comparison notion[16] whereas guilt is not. A child at school may feel shame when he cannot contribute a dime to the Red Cross Fund Drive because his family cannot afford the contribution. When he compares his family to others, he feels that is it not as good as other children's.

Regret is the subjective experience of feeling bad or sorry about the "difference between the outcomes of a chosen versus an unchosen option."[17] A person may regret that she unsuccessfully tried to save a drowning friend by swimming to her when throwing a ring buoy might possibly have saved her life.

All three feelings can erupt when a person experiences a situation that she cannot forgive. For example, if you stole money from your boss and experienced guilt, you might not able to forgive yourself. If you were not as brave as your brother and could not enter a burning house to save a child, you may feel ashamed and not be able to forgive yourself for being less than your brother. The woman who swam unsuccessfully to her drowning friend may also find self-forgiveness almost impossible. She regrets her decision. All three—guilt, shame, and regret—relate directly to who we are and the choices we make. Any one or all three may be felt acutely or chronically by someone who cannot forgive herself.

Grief is, in some ways, a feeling unlike the other three. *Grief* is a person's subjective experience of feeling bad about a loss.[18] The loss can be of a person, a relationship, or even something non-material, like a dream or belief. The difference between grief and the other feelings is that grief need not have any connection with the action or characteristics of the person who expresses it. We grieve the death of loved ones, but have no direct involvement in these deaths. However, when grief is related to self-forgiveness, the grieving person's loss is tied somehow to his actions or characteristics. The woman who regrets not throwing her friend a ring buoy to save the friend's life not only regrets her decision, but she also grieves the loss of her friend. When she begins to forgive herself, she will have to struggle with both feelings, not just one.

A person who needs to forgive herself feels bad because she transgressed a moral rule, fell short of her expectation of herself, made bad decisions, or lost something dear. While any of these feelings may be hard for a person to bear, they also are positive, because they prompt a person to attempt self-forgiveness.

Summary

If you need to forgive yourself, you may be experiencing sorrow, contrition, guilt, and possibly something else. You experience separateness from other people. When we hurt people and remain unforgiven by them, it is as if a door has closed between ourselves and others. We are locked outside alone, unable to go back in. But the greater door closed is the one we close on ourselves: People who have not forgiven themselves are figuratively locked away from others and from themselves. Self-forgiveness is a journey of personal transformation that allows a person to reaccept himself and be reaccepted by others. Limitations previously unrecognized will be exposed in the process. Excuses will be put aside. Admissions will be made that we can and do intentionally hurt others for our own benefit. Self-forgiveness is not related to whether the person whom you hurt has forgiven you. Even if you have been so fortunate, you may recognize that you have a lifelong pattern of letting personal blindness to your flaws result in harm to others.

Forgiving yourself is not about feeling good, or even necessarily about "healing." It is, however, about enormous personal growth brought about by self-examination, honesty, humility, and great personal effort. Self-forgiveness does not just happen; it does not come about either as a result of meditation or "liking yourself more" or seeing your physical self in a more realistic light. Self-forgiveness requires great personal work whether you have lied to a spouse and destroyed your marriage; killed someone because you were drunk; lost a friend because you were disloyal; estranged yourself from your parents or your children because you abused them verbally; damaged your children because you stayed too long in an abusive relationship; or lost a job because you cheated. Self-forgivers refuse to affix to themselves a "victim" label that exonerates them from personal responsibilities. Instead, they accept full responsibility for the losses their actions or inactions have brought them.

At the heart of the human psyche lies the ability to deny our faults and to see ourselves as blameless. Viewing ourselves somewhat inaccurately protects most of us from the raw truth of our own shortcomings. Our shortcomings may cause us great personal hurt; but when they cross over into damaging others, we must learn to forgive ourselves. The decision to forgive yourself means that you will rethink your basic beliefs about yourself and other people. You will attempt to empower yourself through confronting yourself honestly and putting down some of your defenses. Self-forgiveness means that you will reach out to other people and attempt to make amends. Finally, self-forgiveness may result in greater self-acceptance. It most surely results in a transformation of who you are and how you affect others. In all likelihood, once you have forgiven yourself, you will look back in amazement that you ever accepted yourself and were blind to who and what you really were.

At the end of the process of self-forgiveness, you will feel free from self-loathing, free of the nagging sense of indebtedness to others, hopeful about the future, and clear about the moral stances you take in your life. The process is one of hope. At its end lies a life transformation you may have been seeking for years.

PART I

Your Own Worst Enemy: The Challenge of Self-Forgiveness

MANY of life's critical decisions result in wounded feelings and damaged relationships. If you have had to decide to leave a ruinous marriage or place an infirm parent in a nursing home or inform a dear friend of her husband's shady business dealings, you know all too well that these kinds of decisions, no matter how they are finalized, hurt someone. You may also be a person whose limitations, mistakes, or wrongdoings contributed to harming someone. But not all transgressions and mistakes result in suffering or call for self-forgiveness.

When do you need to forgive yourself? When do you not? Imagine that you had to make a decision to put your adolescent daughter's baby up for adoption because neither you nor she could care for it. You feel you made the best decision for everyone, but your daughter says that she hates you. Do you need to forgive yourself? Or imagine that you cannot forgive yourself for saying something truthful to a friend that saved her job but was so painful for her to hear that you lost her friendship. You, like many who are not sure about forgiveness, feel right and wrong at the same time. Part of you seeks forgiveness and self-forgiveness, and the other part believes that you are being held accountable unjustifiably.

How do you decide if self-forgiveness is necessary? Part I of *Forgiving Yourself* addresses this question. If you cause harm to others, do you need to forgive yourself? If others say you are hurting them, do you need to forgive yourself? If you violate an agreement that you had no part in designing, is forgiveness warranted? Some readers may decide, after reading Part I, that they have been struggling to forgive themselves when there is nothing to forgive. Others may conclude that they must face the challenge of self-forgiveness. If you decide that there is nothing to forgive yourself for, you are free to put away shame and guilt and move forward. If, on the other hand, you decide that you need to forgive yourself, you can do the hard work of freeing yourself from self-reproach so that you can look to the future with hope, rather than being a slave to your past mistakes. If you have been your own worst enemy, now may be the time to transform yourself into a friend—by forgiving yourself.

CHAPTER 1

Do You Need to Forgive Yourself?

Barbara Bowman and her husband, Lawrence, went to bed after a peaceful evening of watching television. They lived in a prosperous suburb, had many friends, and their thirty-year marriage and family life was considered a model of the American Dream. All that changed with a telephone call at 2:00 A.M. informing the Bowmans that the eldest of their four children, Nathan, had been found dead of an overdose in the boulevard of a busy street not too far from their home. The couple found it hard to identify their son: the once handsome twenty-seven-year-old was emaciated and clad in near-rags, so unlike the child they had known.

For the next decade, even though Barbara threw herself into her community activities, she was racked by guilt and a sense of failure. Her marriage nearly ended—it could hardly bear the weight of her grief. Because of her fear that she had somehow contributed to Nathan's death, Mrs. Bowman's sense of her past, future, and self were severely compromised by his fatal overdose.

Katherine ran for the kitchen drawer. With her right hand, she fumbled for the scissors, while she tried with her left to force Dave's knife away from her body. She could smell the stench of booze. Her husband's eyes flared with the rage of some savage beast cornered by a gunman against a wire fence. Katherine felt the handles of the scissors and secured them around her thumb and third finger. She clutched them firmly, took a sliding step forward, and drove the scissors into his thigh.

Sally, seven, and John, five, screamed helplessly nearby as their father bellowed in surprise and crashed into the fully set dinner table. Katherine told the children to run outside where she could see them out of the corner of her eye. Like a wild animal guarding its young from danger she rushed toward the man she had married ten years earlier. Then she saw that Dave had passed out. Katherine put the children into the car and drove to the battered women's shelter as she had two times before. The last time, she entered with a gashed lip and a broken arm. Before that, it was two crushed ribs. This time, she walked into the facility with only resolve as her wound. This time, she was going to begin the process of divorcing Dave.

The stories of Barbara Bowman and Katherine Miller reflect the deep pain of people who believe they need to forgive themselves. Both women, when I interviewed them, expressed anger, deep grief, regret, and self-condemnation. But the two women had come to different conclusions about self-forgiveness. One decided she wanted desperately to go through the self-forgiveness process described in Part II of this book. The other decided she did not. Barbara concluded after much soul searching that, while she believed at first that she was responsible for Nathan's death, she really was not. Katherine, by contrast, concluded that she was at least partially responsible for the psychological damage done to her children; and so, she faced the challenge of self-forgiveness. What are the differences between these women? Both blamed themselves for their children's wounds. Both had tried to protect their children from harm. Both had made mistakes in their marriages and parenting; and both had obvious shortcomings. So why did they draw different conclusions about self-forgiveness? More generally, when do people need to forgive themselves? In what circumstances do people who once believed they needed to forgive themselves decide that they do not?

Some answers to these questions lie in the very ways that people injure each other. How we hurt each other and subsequently suffer contrition, guilt, helplessness, or regret reveals whether self-forgiveness is appropriate in our lives.

How People Hurt Each Other: Direct and Indirect Injuries

How do we really know when we are responsible for hurting another person; that is, how can a person know that it is her limitations, transgressions, or mistakes that actually harm someone, and are not the limitations, transgressions, or mistakes of someone else? The answers lie, in part, in the notions of direct and indirect injuries. We hurt each other directly when we shoot, push, shove, kick, slap, or stab another. Or we may demean, lie to, humiliate, shame, or excoriate others. When people do these things to others, they cause direct injuries. Conversely, those who sustain these injuries have been wounded directly by another person. A mother who slaps her child has committed a direct injury. She may justify this action by telling herself that, had she not hit the child, her husband would have later. If her husband does slap the child later, there are two direct injuries. Even if direct injuries are similar, they are not interchangeable.

All injuries done to people directly are not necessarily matters where self-forgiveness is important. An executioner directly injures the one he kills, but he probably does not experience guilt, remorse, or contrition.

In the introduction, we said that self-forgiveness is in order when people's behavior not only hurts others, but also alters an injurer's central life assumptions and the quality of his or her life. The executioner may cause direct harm, but he experiences no emotional difficulties as a result.

People who directly injure others and experience a need to be forgiven not only wound others and feel terrible about it, they share another similarity. They probably could have known ahead of time that their behavior or actions would harm someone. The woman who slapped her child did not intend to loosen one of his teeth, but she did. She cannot forgive herself because she knows that she could have foreseen that her slap might do more than she had intended. A slap is just too difficult to control to be able to predict its outcome.

The man who backs his car out of the garage over a neighbor's visiting grandchild at play may believe he should have been able to foresee the accident. He feels he cannot "forgive" himself, but he is coming to share the conviction of his family and friends that—because he could not have known the child would be there (the child had never visited before)—he experienced a terrible accident, but does not need to go through the difficult self-exploration that self-forgiveness requires.

Direct injuries that cause people to need self-forgiveness are those, then, that would involve actions that have a clearly harmful effect on others that might be anticipated. In addition, when direct injuries occur, one person probably could have foreseen that her behavior would result in injury to another person. Many, but by no means all, of the circumstances that cause a person to be unable to forgive himself are results of direct injuries. Others are results of indirect injuries. Barbara Bowman and Katherine Miller are different from one another because one caused an indirect injury to her child, and the other caused a direct injury.

Indirect injuries are different from direct injuries in two very critical ways. In an indirect injury, harm that happens to a wounded person may result from the participation, involvement, or actual existence of another person; and that person may or may not be able to foresee that, because of his participation or involvement in an incident, harm will occur.

For example, the person who issued the launch command for the space shuttle *Challenger* was indirectly involved in the astronauts' deaths when their rocket exploded. The launch commander's position in a causal line of responsibility from "most responsible" to "least responsible," however, was very low. In fact, had he called in sick the morning of the launch and another person had given the launch command, the same tragedy would have occurred. He, as a person, was replaceable, but the event would still have taken place. A person who suspects that she may have participated in another person's injury can trace her steps backward from the injury and then identify the necessity of her involvement or the place of importance of her specific contribution to it.

When an indirect injury occurs, the injurer realizes that she may have participated in the harm, but more than likely could not have foreseen or altered the fact that it would result in tragedy. This is Barbara Bowman's situation. When she tracked backward from Nathan's death to look for any contribution she made to his life that might have contributed to his death, she could not identify any. She considered that, had she not been responsible for three other children, she might have been a better mother and he may not have turned to drugs. She wondered if it were genetic (although her other children are well-adjusted and productive members of society). Barbara could establish no clear link between herself and Nathan's death except that she had been his mother. No clear limitation, mistake, or transgression emerged as a necessary antecedent to his overdose. At one time in her painful search she even debated whether her refusal to buy Nathan a new suit might have played a part:

> *"I remembered when he came home all excited in the seventh grade, I think, and wanted a new suit. I couldn't imagine what for so I said, 'We don't have the money to buy all kinds of suits. What is it for?'*
>
> *"When he said it was because he wanted to take some girl to a dance I said, 'We buy suits to go to church, not to take girls to dances.'*

> *"For a long time when I thought of him lying dead, I said to myself over and over, 'Why couldn't you have just bought him the suit?'"*

Barbara Bowman's search for any direct or indirect injury she caused Nathan continued for several years. She began to wonder, as much as it frightened her, if she had been removed from the situation altogether, would her son's life still have ended so prematurely and sadly? To find answers, she decided to go to the police station and talk with officers. What she found was shocking.

Nathan had begun to push heroin several years before his death. A woman with whom he shot up and who might have given him his fatal overdose had injected too large a dose in him before. He had been transported to the emergency room several times before, a fact not known to Barbara or Lawrence. She was also informed that Nathan's arrest record was lengthy and that the police had been aware of his ascension up the drug-dealing ladder where he disbursed all kinds of drugs to an ever-enlarging geographical area.

As she learned the painful truth about her son, she began to regard her questions about herself in a new light.

Barbara remembered taking Nathan to a counselor when she and Lawrence discovered his marijuana use when he was thirteen. She recalled her painful attempts to enact "tough love" with Nathan when she and her husband made a decision not to allow him to come home because he posed a danger to their other children. She remembered the pain of rescuing him from jail, paying for drug treatments that did not work, and realizing, in tears, that it was Nathan who stole her jewelry, not a burglar. Finally, Barbara concluded:

> *"There are things much worse than death. The pain will always be a part of me. But I don't have a negative view of myself anymore. I've changed my values and how I judge myself.*

"I realized—finally—that I did not cause his death. I wasn't a bad person. He had made some extremely poor choices as an adult. He hated himself."

As sad as Mrs. Bowman's conclusion was, it was liberating. She decided that she caused Nathan no direct harm. She also decided that if she had caused him indirect harm, it was minimal: For his death to have happened, his birth had to have happened. So, in that way and a few others, Barbara decided that she was indirectly involved in Nathan's death, just as the launch commander was indirectly involved in the *Challenger* explosion. At the time of both tragedies, either person could have been taken out of the picture, yet the tragedies would have still occurred. For all the pain Barbara Bowman experienced, she could not attach any clear personal transgression, mistake, or limitation to her loss. She had kept her promises to Nathan, tried to protect him, attempted to understand him, and never deserted him. She still grieves, but she is no longer seeking self-forgiveness.

Katherine Miller, by contrast, arrived at far different conclusions from Mrs. Bowman's; and Katherine's conclusions will put her at the gateway of the process of self-forgiveness described in Part II.

KATHERINE'S CONCLUSIONS ABOUT HER CHILDREN'S INJURIES

Katherine Miller's children, Sally, seven, and John, five, had witnessed many incidents of violence in their young lives. They had watched as her husband, Dave, pounded her with his fists to the floor of their kitchen while she begged for mercy.

They had seen her in the hospital with bruised eye sockets and a broken pelvis after one of Dave's drunken rampages. When Sally had tried one time to step between her violent parents, Katherine screamed at her to leave the room. Katherine's children know how to dial 911. They have seen the inside of the battered women's shelter. Sally suffers from headaches and anxiety attacks. She sometimes sleeps in her closet. She yells out during her frequent nightmares. John stutters. He occasionally wets the bed. At times he has bowel incontinence, for which he is deeply ashamed.

Katherine is a victim, by any standards. Yet, she searches for self-forgiveness despite protests from women in the battered women's shelter, her parents, and especially her friends. "You did all you could to protect the children," they tell her; but Katherine has assessed her participation in Sally's and John's psychological injuries differently from her well-intentioned supporters. Katherine believes that even if she had not hit or slapped Sally and John, as Dave beat her, she did directly injure them just as surely as she was injured, but in a different way.

Why does Katherine hold herself accountable for her children's direct injuries while Barbara cannot? What are the differences in their circumstances?

Katherine has decided that her role in the violence her children witnessed between her and Dave reflects specific aspects of her personality, especially the ways that she responds to violence and conflict. Another woman's responses to violence might have had a completely different impact on the same children.

Katherine had always been inconsistent in her reaction to Dave's beatings. Sometimes she begged. Other times she ran away or hit him back. At times she screamed; at other times she cried. She began to see that, to Sally and John, she must have seemed as inconsistent and volatile as their father.

Katherine also concluded that she could have foreseen that her children would be harmed, and yet did not take action to prevent such harm. She had been an elementary education major before she left school to marry. She had taken courses in the psychology of young children and understood the impact of violence on children, including domestic violence. Still, she participated in the violence rather than leaving it. She holds herself accountable for causing direct harm to her children, but she is unable to isolate the exact source of her contribution to her children's injuries. She cannot determine if she did something wrong, had a specific limitation that hurt her children, or if she simply made a mistake.

To identify the source of her children's wounds, Katherine, like all people who decide they need to forgive themselves, will have to trace back from the injury to any of her transgressions, limitations, or mistakes to see if they did, indeed, contribute to the harm of another—in this case, her own children.

KATHERINE'S TRANSGRESSIONS WITH DAVE

Katherine began to explore the ways she could have transgressed a moral agreement with Dave. She knew she had not lied to him, or had affairs, or broken promises. But somehow violence had become an integral part of their relationship. Katherine wondered how this could have happened and began to reflect on her moral history with Dave.

Moral histories are like other histories that people share. As people get to know each other and spend time together, they develop a history of shared experiences and events. A critical part of this history is how they determine together what is morally acceptable or unacceptable in their relationship. The determination of right and wrong between friends, partners, or parents and children is made as these people face, and then solve, moral questions that challenge them. If one person solves a personal moral question, the other can observe the solution and offer his opinion of it. If two people together solve a moral dilemma, they can discuss the situation as they attempt to find solutions and observe each other's process of thinking. Right and wrong are defined continually in a relationship. These definitions become the substance of people's moral lives and moral histories together.

During Katherine and Dave's ten years of marriage, Dave had helped Katherine decide whether to encourage the removal of her grandmother's respirator as she lay near death. They agreed that it was the merciful and moral thing to do. Early in their marriage, when Dave had flirted with a friend and Katherine had protested, the couple ruled that flirting was unacceptable in each other's presence. When Katherine learned that Dave was going to cheat on their joint tax return, she protested. They debated, negotiated, and decided to be honest. When

Katherine hit a parked car and was going to drive away without leaving a note on the windshield, Dave encouraged her to do so.

Katherine and Dave's moral history was complex (as most are); and while the couple had solved many moral questions, they had not solved the question of whether violence would be tolerated in their relationship. Dave had transgressed his marriage vow to Katherine, and when he hit her, he did not honor her. He had committed a crime. Katherine, however, had not transgressed her moral agreement with Dave. When she left for good, she finally made it clear that violence was, to her, morally unacceptable. Before then, however, she had sent many mixed signals. She loved her husband, was dependent on him financially, and believed in the sanctity of marriage vows. She also wanted her children to not be estranged from their father.

KATHERINE'S TRANSGRESSION OF HER MORAL RESPONSIBILITIES TO HER CHILDREN

Most of us have competing moral claims on us. Katherine was no exception. While she and Dave negotiated the moral rules that would govern their relationship, other moral relationships in her life were continuing to evolve. Katherine expected loyalty from her best friend, for example. They had always supported each other. When the friend first told her that she was becoming uncomfortable with their friendship because she feared that her support of Katherine made it easier for her to return to Dave, Katherine did not take serious notice. Next, her friend strongly urged her to leave him for the children's sake. When she chose not to and returned to Dave after a beating, the friend ended their relationship. She could no longer accept Katherine's definition of what constituted an acceptable marital relationship.

Katherine was also developing an evolving moral relationship with her children. They were able to watch her negotiate right and wrong. If John and Sally were not fully capable of knowing right from wrong because they were too young, Katherine was capable. Like most parents, she believed that she had a special obligation to protect her children from harm and to demonstrate values she believed were right, such as honesty and loyalty. A problem evolved, however, when she demonstrated loyalty to Dave (that is, when she did not leave him). She at the same time failed to protect her children from witnessing terrible violence and, therefore, on some level abandoned them. She knew the impact these observations were having on Sally and John and finally recognized that all the while she had tried to negotiate the moral terms in her marriage, she had violated a competing moral obligation to her children. Even though she was a victim of direct harm, her participation in continuing violence directly wounded her children. Unlike Barbara Bowman, Katherine is beginning to see that without her specific participation in her ongoing victimization and her unwillingness to stop it, her children would not have been wounded. They, unlike Mrs. Bowman's children, were wounded because of their mother's failure to meet a moral obligation to them.

For this, Katherine must try to forgive herself. Katherine also recognizes that there were underlying reasons she did not leave her violent situation. These reasons lay in the limitations she brought with her into her marriage.

KATHERINE'S LIMITATION

Katherine knows that, in addition to not meeting her moral obligation to protect her children, she has a dangerous limitation that contributed to her children's suffering.

A limitation was defined in the introduction as a restrictive weakness. Katherine's weakness that restricted her judgment about leaving her violent marriage was this: She believed secretly that she was a kind of "healer." She had thought, because she was young, that her love was special and could repair damaged people. She was drawn to friends and other people who reinforced her belief. When she met Dave, she learned that he had had a difficult childhood. She committed herself to helping him to overcome its impact; so when she realized that her love was not diminishing his violent outbursts, she tried to love him even better. Dave was challenging one of Katherine's central beliefs. So Katherine rose to the challenge.

Over the years when it became clearer to her that she could not "fix" Dave with "ordinary" love, she placed herself in a position to sustain her husband's rage and then comfort him. When she could provide comfort, she could believe again that her love was special. Katherine's concept of love was tangled with ideas about repairing people for the better. This limited idea of love did not change, despite evidence to the contrary. Katherine could not reject her ideas about her love's healing powers though they were not supported by facts. She described her desire to "help" Dave with this explanation:

> "I wanted always to help my husband even before I helped myself. It was the way I was raised. See, my mother worshipped my father. Dad did what he wanted when he wanted. But he didn't drink. My husband's dad, though, was an alcoholic. So are his mom and all his brothers. I felt sorry for my husband, and still do. He's tried hard, but maybe he could have tried harder. I figured . . . if I made my husband more important than myself, I could do more for him and with him. He was more important to me than he is to himself. He really doesn't think he is worth much, and I wanted to correct that. In fact, I think I can take the credit for some of the changes he's making now."

Katherine's limitation, her intractable conviction that her love would one day extinguish Dave's rage, finally collided directly with her growing awareness that her faulty idea of love was causing her children great harm.

Katherine knows that, even though she is a victim, she contributed directly to her children's psychological damage. She has been able to trace their confusion, fears, and physical symptoms directly to two personal sources: her failure to protect her children and her lifelong inability or unwillingness to accept the limits of her love. For her transgressions and limitations she will try to forgive herself.

Mrs. Bowman now knows that Nathan would have died even if she had lived elsewhere or had been dead herself. He began his drug use so early in his life that, regardless of the Bowmans' deep love and futile attempts to help him, the inevitable course of his life took a predictable pathway. Mrs. Bowman will always feel a hollow spot in her heart; but she does not need to try to forgive herself anymore. People who try to forgive themselves must make significant personal changes during which they resolve to not transgress moral agreements and to alter any personal limitations that have caused harm to other people. Mrs. Bowman does not need to make specific personal changes. Katherine Miller does.

Do You Need to Forgive Yourself?

When you directly, or even indirectly, hurt someone, you may choose to engage in the difficult process of forgiving yourself.

The direct harm you caused might have stemmed from losing your temper and belittling, humiliating, or hitting someone, thereby transgressing a moral agreement. Or you may have violated a law and caused another person a direct physical injury.

You may have indirectly injured another person when you failed to improve a limitation that would likely result in harm to another.

If you are like Barbara Bowman and conclude that you were not necessary to another person's injury, you may feel grief or loss, but have no need to go through a process of self-examination and self-disclosure that forgiving yourself requires. If on the other hand, you, like Katherine Miller, can link your limitations, transgressions, or mistakes to another person's wounds, you may decide to commit yourself to the process of personal transformation intrinsic to self-forgiveness. Only if you can determine that you need to forgive yourself, will it be possible for you to attempt it.

CHAPTER 2

Meeting Our Limitations

All his life Jonas believed that he was a natural woodsman, an outdoorsman beyond ordinary talent. He marched his children through forests, pointing out that moss grew on the south side of trees, when they had learned in Boy Scouts that moss grew on the north side. He identified the evening primrose as a yellow jasmine even when his wife, Julie, somewhat of a wildflower expert, attempted to show him the difference between the two flowers. He wrongly identified cumulus and stratocumulus clouds. Yet when people attempted to correct or argue with Jonas, his unawareness of his basic limitations coupled with his stubborn arrogance resulted in his dismissing other people's opinions, no matter how expert another person might be.

One spring, Jonas decided to take Julie and the boys to the Rocky Mountains for an early-season hike. The snow was barely off the foothills, but Jonas insisted it was the right time to see the mountain juncos arrive in the Rockies. The morning was blustery, but Jonas had determined from his search of the sky that no snow was to fall. Julie had seen on the Weather Channel, though, that a snow squall was predicted for that afternoon. But against her arguments and in spite of his children's protests, Jonas and family set out into the forests below the alpine level where Jonas hoped to see the juncos.

Three hours into the hike it began to snow. Several inches of snow were on the ground in an hour. The trail was quickly obscured under the white blanket. Because the family had not prepared for wet weather, they had carried no rain gear. Wet skin, even Jonas knew, could be a catastrophe for hikers. Hypothermia had killed many in the Rockies. The terrified family hiked on. As the snow continued to fall, Jonas and Julie covered what they could of their children's exposed skin with their own sweaters and tried to calm their increasing terror as they staggered down the mountain. After a short time, the youngest boy's skin turned white, and his body began to shake uncontrollably. Julie knew that these were signs of hypothermia, and with quick thinking, stripped the boy of his wet clothes, took him inside her sweater so that his skin was next to hers, and asked Jonas for his windbreaker to put around the two of them. She instructed Jonas to build a fire to melt snow for a warm liquid to give the shaking little boy. Jonas had never been successful at building fires when wood was wet, and, for once, he managed to admit his limitation to Julie. She told him and the other two boys to fold their arms over their chests and bend together to form a "tent" over her and the boy.

Fortunately, moments later a cross-country skier spotted the cluster of people. When the little boy's shaking body quieted after being given some warm liquid, the skier led the wet, cold party to the nearby parking lot where their van was parked. Jonas drove the family to a hospital. His son was treated and released from the emergency room. He still does not know, though, whether the frostbite another son contracted in his fingers and toes will result in permanent loss of feeling in the boy's hands and feet.

❧❧

In some ways, Jonas's near tragedy may seem to be more a result of a mistake, or a series of mistakes, than a result of some personal limitation. It may seem a mistake, for example, to have gone on a hike too early in the season, or a mistake not to have paid attention to the weather report. If Jonas does not confront himself honestly after his family's close call with tragedy, he might inaccurately tell himself that what happened was an unhappy series of circumstances; but Jonas knows better. So do Julie and the boys. They know that Jonas's limitations, both in his knowledge and his incapacity to see himself as he really is, nearly cost them their lives.

Unrecognized limitations are perhaps the most common source of injuries people cannot forgive themselves for, even more common than injuries resulting from mistakes or wrongdoings. Because people's limitations—whether innate or acquired—are often hidden, and because our psychological makeups provide us with tools that assist us in not seeing ourselves as we are, a tragedy or near-tragedy might have to occur to force someone to confront her shortcomings. In a sense, a person's capacity to deny, forget, or repress her flaws is mirrored by her capacity to deny, repress, or forget the flaws of others.

The illusions people create about themselves and other people make it easier for us to get along. When a person's limitations, though, become so dangerous that they are no longer hidden, then that person will have to reassess herself, which often precipitates the need for self-forgiveness. This is Jonas's situation. He cannot forget what he did; he cannot repress it. When he sees his older son's fingers continue to darken, he still worries about amputations. Jonas knows he cannot marshal the strategies that previously allowed him to believe that he is smarter, more knowledgeable, or better than he truly is. He is limited; and his lack of awareness of his limitations almost killed someone.

Limitations, where self-forgiveness is concerned, must be examined very carefully. They must be sorted through and analyzed critically, so that people do not blame themselves and hate themselves for limitations that are not real. One of life's most difficult tasks is to confront oneself honestly about personal flaws. It is equally difficult for a person to sort out his real limitations from characteristics that other people may not like, but that harm no one.

Real Limitations and False Limitations

Many people struggle to "forgive" themselves when there is nothing to forgive. People believe that their limited intelligence, a strength, or an insight hurt someone else unforgivably when nothing could be farther from the truth.

Sarah, a middle-aged woman similar to Katherine, had also been battered for years. Sarah considered leaving her marriage and sought her mother's counsel. Her mother had also lived with a batterer all her life and convinced Sarah that she had a serious flaw—selfishness. Selfishness, the mother said, was tempting Sarah to leave her abusive marriage. Over several years of such convincing, Sarah came to believe that she should forgive herself for letting the shortcoming of self-centeredness affect her relationship. She then tried to change herself in a futile attempt to subdue her husband's violence. Sarah was, ironically, anything but selfish.

Selfishness for Sarah is a false limitation, and her belief in this false limitation leads to faulty life assumptions, which prohibit her from leaving an abusive marriage. People who struggle to forgive themselves must see what it is about themselves they really need to forgive. When they can see this clearly, they will identify the real mistakes, limitations, and wrongdoings that have harmed others and themselves. The distinction between false and real is vital to the forgiving process because people must know what it is they are attempting to forgive. What is the difference between real and false limitations?

1. False limitations, unlike real ones, are defined by people other than those who have the "limitations." By contrast, real limitations become apparent to a person who has hurt someone else because of those limitations.
2. False limitations are used to manipulate people. Especially, they are used by people who claim to be injured in an effort to manipulate the "injurer" to change a behavior or attitude in a way that would be advantageous to the "injured."
3. False limitations are not necessarily obvious to people outside a relationship. Other people who observe the relationship between a "flawed" person and the one who claims to be injured cannot see any connection between the flaw and the injury.

Let's apply these three points to Sarah's situation:

1. Sarah was branded as selfish by her mother and her husband.
2. Both gained advantages if Sarah believed this about herself. Her abusive husband would not be deserted, and her mother would keep Sarah as a kindred spirit who had also suffered abuse.
3. No one saw Sarah as selfish except her mother and her husband; indeed, she was considered entirely unselfish by almost everyone who knew her.

Sarah will have to tease out her real flaws from her false ones if she is to begin to forgive herself, otherwise she will attempt to forgive herself for the wrong reasons. The same is true for Cheryl.

THE DANGER OF FALSE LIMITATIONS

Cheryl's lifelong self-hatred, which grew out of her perceived "limitation" of being unable to understand her father, has all the earmarks of a false limitation.

Cheryl, now thirty-six, still blames herself for her incestuous relationship with her father. She has been to many therapists and support groups, but still feels no anger toward her father. Instead, she hates herself.

Cheryl's father began to sexually stimulate her when she was about five. Her body betrayed her when the stimulation felt good. About two years later, her father began to tell her how lonely he was. If the little girl resisted his advances, he told her she was not trying to understand him. Then he would cry. When he cried, the confused child felt as though she had failed him, so she increased her efforts to please and gave in to his sexual pressuring. The manipulation continued like this for several more years. At puberty when Cheryl began to really resist, her father blamed her for his problems with her mother. Cheryl finally told her mother. Ultimately, a divorce followed, and her father was incarcerated.

Cheryl holds herself responsible for both. To this day, Cheryl thinks that she should have understood her father's deep sadness and helped him somehow. She believes that had she been a more understanding person, this might not have happened to her or to their family.

Cheryl's molestations had nothing to do with her shortcomings or flaws. They had to do with her father's psychological and moral problems.

Everyone in Cheryl's life has told her that her father's abusive behavior had nothing to do with her; but she is locked in a complex, erroneous, yet *internally* logical belief pattern. She knows that being "kinder" to him resulted in her own molestation. Yet being "unkind" resulted in his tears and self-degradation. Cheryl believes she chose to be molested over seeing him be unhappy. He still believes he did nothing wrong. In his view, his psychological manipulation of her made both of them happy.

The false limitations felt by Cheryl have all three of the characteristics mentioned earlier. The supposedly "injured" person defined the limitation. Her father manipulated her belief in her "limitations" to his own benefit, convincing Cheryl that she was responsible for his problems. Other people cannot see that Cheryl's failures had anything whatsoever to do with her assaults. Cheryl has nothing to forgive herself for, but she will need much help to convince herself of this.

Marietta thought that her limitations ruined her marriage. Actually, they had nothing to do with her marriage troubles. Her husband's sexual appetites brought the marriage to an end.

⌘

Marietta knew even before she was married that she had trouble with her weight and that her cooking skills were limited. Six months after her wedding, Jose had an affair with a younger, thinner woman. When Marietta confronted Jose, he told her that she was fat and that her weight turned him off.

Marietta went on a crash diet to improve herself and make herself more attractive. After another year or so, she had lost twenty pounds and learned to apply her makeup more skillfully. Her friends told her she looked beautiful. Then Marietta learned that Jose was having another affair. This time, he told her it was her fault because she could not cook him a good meal. Marietta could not forgive herself for failing Jose. She asked him to "forgive" her for not trying hard enough to improve.

After five years of this, and because she was a strong woman, Marietta managed to leave Jose with some degree of

*her self-esteem intact. She knew she had shortcomings; but she
also saw that no matter how hard she tried to work on her perceived limitations, Jose was dissatisfied with her. Instead of
struggling for the rest of her life to please him and to "forgive"
herself, she recognized there was nothing to forgive. Jose had
problems, and he needed help. She, however, could not solve
the problems for him.*

Being in a relationship in which you are constantly being apprised of
your limitations by someone else and struggling always to "forgive"
yourself is like being on a boat sailing toward the western horizon; but as
you sail, the horizon keeps receding from you. People who falsely perceive themselves as falling short or who are plagued with externally
imposed limitations also pursue "receding" horizons. They can never
reach their goals of improving enough to please someone because that
goal is always unattainable. Anyone who has tried to please or show
loyalty to a person who is never satisfied knows how it feels to not
"be enough." There is no way to ever "improve" enough to finally
be "acceptable."

Most people try to please other people. Pleasing and being pleased
makes us attractive to each other. We try to look good to please each
other; we try to be understanding or generous. Being a part of something
larger than ourselves is vital to our self-concepts, physical well-being,
and emotional stability. We are social animals who want to belong. The
lucky among us find ways to please the people we care for and are appre-
ciated for our efforts without being manipulated. The unlucky—that is,
the battered children, abused spouses, emotionally abused, or shamed
among us—find that no matter what they do, they cannot please. Yet
they still try. False limitations followed by self-degradation and non-
forgiveness must be examined for validity. If upon examination limitations prove to be false, a person needs to seek help to understand the
complex ways these limitations have been bestowed by manipulation.

If you find yourself not able to "forgive" yourself in a continuing situation where you cannot do enough for someone else, ask yourself these questions:

Are these "limitations" pointed out to you, for the most part, by the other person or people you turn to for support?

Is the injury "caused" by your "limitation" an injury your friends or family members connect to that perceived limitation?

Have you tried to improve your shortcomings, but no matter how hard you try, you are still told you are hurting this other person?

If you answer "yes" to any of these questions, you may have inadvertently become locked into a situation where you will find no way to feel better about yourself. Your "limitations" are being used as weapons to keep you subservient to, or in some other way beholden to, someone else to whom you can never fully pay your "debt." You have nothing to forgive yourself for, but you will have to work hard to extricate yourself from this imbalanced bondage. False limitations, innate or acquired, tether people to abusive, unhappy, or even dangerous relationships.

Not living up to someone else's standards is not unforgivable. Just as one person can try to improve herself where there are shortcomings in character or abilities, another person can change her standards. Adults who experience false limitations may have come from families in which there was physical or emotional abuse. If this is your case, it will not be easy to free yourself from the pattern of attempting to please another person who judges and manipulates you; if you must forgive yourself, though, it will result from a careful analysis of what, if anything, you have done that requires forgiveness.

Real Limitations That Cause Non-Forgiveness

When people hurt others, permanently damage relationships, or destroy their bedrock assumptions because of some personal shortcoming, the pain is immense.

We might be able to forgive ourselves for doing wrong, but it is more humbling to forgive ourselves for letting one of our flaws result in irreparable damage. This is Jonas's situation. He must assess and then accept the fact that his illusions about himself went unheeded and unchecked for too long. To forgive himself, Jonas must confront himself for the first time and recognize that his inflated sense of himself endangers the people he loves. When he can identify what it is he needs to forgive, he can then engage in personal transformation. All who need to forgive themselves must first see themselves for what they are, and then commit to making substantial changes.

TRUE LIMITATIONS

In general, limitations that erupt into unforgivable situations are limitations in recognizing personal traits that may cause harm or failing to recognize limitations in competency. A person may know that she is weak, opinionated, stubborn, possessive, jealous, or too prone to intruding into other people's private lives, but she does not recognize how ruinous these traits may be until damage occurs. This happened to both Jonas and Katherine. Some people cannot recognize their areas of incompetence, and others are unable to recognize their thresholds of incompetence. Dave, an accomplished trumpeter, had trouble recognizing his threshold of incompetence.

Dave tried out for a local television talent show. He won it and then the regional competition by playing "Harlem Nocturne," a classic but not too difficult jazz standard. Two weeks before the state competition, and without consulting with anyone, Dave decided to change his try-out piece. The winner of the state contest was to take home $10,000 and go on to national competition and the chance to be featured on "Star Search" on network TV.

Performing live on statewide cable television, Dave missed the first note. Recovering, but shaky, he completely blew a difficult passage. His lips began to quiver, after which he went blank and stopped in the middle of the performance. Dave was a disaster! He had chosen a much too difficult piece, and because he was not really familiar with it, he could not recover when he began to make mistakes. His family and friends were embarrassed, and Dave was humiliated. He could not "forgive" himself for trying to do something he was not competent to do. Dave was competent to a certain threshold; but once he passed over the threshold, he was not. He revealed his limitations, not only to himself and his friends and family, but also to the entire state.

Fortunately, Dave's gaffe did not permanently harm his relationships or do irreparable damage to other people. In other words, Dave did not have to forgive himself so much as accept himself and simply go forward, a more humble man.

ALTERED RELATIONSHIPS AND APOLOGIES

When people break moral agreements, they are generally aware of the potential consequences of doing so. Liars, cheaters, thieves, and adulterers are not suddenly made aware of areas or thresholds of wrongdoing. They know they are doing something wrong, and they await being caught. Once caught, they may also know how their relationships with the people they betrayed will change.

People with limitations, by contrast, do not recognize the ways that their flaws, once unveiled, will change the people around them. The changes may be much subtler than the changes that occur in relationships wherein people have been betrayed. Jonas's sons are an example. Nick, his oldest boy, now worships his Boy Scout leader, and turns down

Jonas's invitations to camp or hike. The second son has begun to stay after school to be in a science club with a teacher he seems to like. Jonas grieves the fact that he has tumbled from his pedestal and will, in all likelihood, never be placed there again. Julie has also become more willing to argue with him and to make her own decisions when the two of them disagree. Jonas feels worthless. He feels he has fallen short as a person, and he feels vaguely sick about himself.

Jonas apologized over and over again to the boys and to Julie. Each and every time, his apologies were accepted. As in all injuries that require self-forgiveness, though, the apology could not undo the permanent changes in his relationship with his family. Jonas wants to be a hero in the eyes of his family; his apologies will not give him that. Instead of being "hero," he will come to accept himself as a person—good at some things, not so good at others—and hopefully, he will learn that he is loved regardless of his flaws.

Apologies, whether accepted or unaccepted, do not restore relationships to their original form. Jonas's standing with his family members has been permanently changed because of his false perception of himself. And even heartfelt apologies will not negate his need to do the hard work of reaching a true and accurate understanding of himself.

When one of your shortcomings changes your own world, your bedrock beliefs about the world unravel. Jonas believed he was worthy; he believed that the world was a good place. He, like the rest of us, believed that life has a certain predictability, and that we control, to some extent, the occurrences in the personal arenas of our lives.

When a relationship has been damaged, the "injurer" quickly learns that his assumptions about himself can no longer be trusted. The presumed benevolence of the world comes crashing down around an unforgiven situation. The world seems more dangerous and less predictable than before. Jonas now wonders about the meaning of fatherhood. He tried so hard—too hard—to be a hero to his children. Now, as they shut him out, he wonders about the usefulness of all his hard work. He had not been close to his own father, and it causes him great pain to see that his children have lost faith in him. Part of the work of forgiving ourselves is to rebuild assumptions about ourselves and the world that are more realistic. By doing this, we will restore positive and optimistic energy to our damaged relationships.

People who cannot forgive themselves for their limitations ask these kinds of questions:

> *Have I always been blind to my real self? How many other people have I hurt? How many other people have known about me all along? How many of them must think I am a fool?*

Jonas can no longer assume that he is worthy or that he is in control of people's perceptions of him. The same is true for all whose limitations have been suddenly revealed to themselves and to others.

≈✦

Susan had had problems reading since her early days in school. Somehow, though, the teachers passed her along into high school. Even though Susan knew she had begun to "fake" more than she really read, like many others with learning disabilities, she graduated from high school. Susan married soon after high school, and her inability to read caused no harm to anyone until one day her toddler drank some drain cleaner her husband had stored, unbeknownst to Susan, underneath the basement steps. When the child began to scream, Susan could neither read the bottle nor the phone book to find help. The child's gastrointestinal tract was permanently damaged.

Susan's assumptions were destroyed. In one moment, her reading limitations would, for the rest of her life, force her to wonder if she would again injure someone she cared for. She never again assumed that she could control or prevent life's circumstances. Her limitation, exposed suddenly to her loved ones, doctor, clergyman, and herself, changed her view of the world.

≈✦

Assumptions destroyed by a person's shortcomings are agonizing because that person's self-worth is severely damaged while that flaw is being revealed. Naked and exposed, a person cannot restore people's perceptions of him, regardless of effort. But although losing control over your image can be painful, it can also be liberating. A person who sees his flaws and whose flaws are seen no longer needs to concentrate on managing people's perceptions of him. The revelation of a person's limitation may end the habit of self-deception, but it also creates an opportunity for honesty, and honesty is the *sine qua non* of any real personal change, including self-forgiveness.

Wrongdoings, Excuses, and Justifications

Mary Lee looked forward to her counseling sessions with the Reverend Smith. Although she was hurting from her fifteen-year marriage gone stale, she had begun to feel some hopefulness because of the minister's kindness and understanding. Even though he was a very popular and busy man, he always had time to see her; and he did not show disapproval when she mentioned divorce.

At thirty-eight, Mary Lee was weary of her husband Dan's boring lifestyle. All he seemed to do was watch TV, work, and garden. Having no children, Mary Lee felt that she was at a dead end.

One afternoon in a counseling session, Reverend Smith bent over and touched Mary Lee's cheek. Soon after, they became lovers. For the next few months, they had sex every time they met. Mary Lee felt honored, excited, and attractive. She also felt afraid, guilty, and remorseful. She had been taught that a moral person abides by her commitments. A good person keeps promises, tells the truth, and honors her vows.

Reverend Smith had convinced her that her love was a gift, to him, to herself, and to anyone to whom she gave it. He was helping her recognize her gifts, he said, so that she could give them more freely. But Mary Lee, although somewhat convinced, still knew that she was doing something wrong. After six months, she ended the affair, but by that time Dan and many of her friends had found out about it.

A year later, her marriage ended. Her parents were devastated, and her friends were divided. Some abandoned her and sided with Dan. Some believed that she had been terribly vulnerable and had been taken advantage of by the minister. More extreme friends want the reverend ousted from his parish. What started out as a seemingly private decision has destroyed a marriage, a family, friendships, and even part of a community. Transgressions, even those not intended to be discovered, can destroy lives at many levels.

꧁꧂

All transgressions—whether affairs, lies, or stealing—transgress the boundaries of acceptable or unacceptable behavior. Unlike mistakes or limitations, transgressions involve forethought and intent. Mary Lee intended to have sexual relations with Reverend Smith and, in doing so, to violate her marriage vows. She cannot tell herself that she did not do anything wrong because she is a woman of conscience.

Mary Lee could have thought of herself as Reverend Smith's victim. In fact, she was. People are victims when they are taken advantage of by others who have more strength or power than they do and at a time when they are especially vulnerable. Laws in almost every state make it a felony for a therapist to have sexual relations with a client, and professional codes of ethics forbid the practice. Mary Lee could easily have regarded herself as a foil, and professional friends would have quickly assured her that her conclusion was correct. However, Mary Lee had a problem. The problem for her and for many of us who fall prey to other people when we are vulnerable, was that she could not convince herself that she played no part in the affair. She felt terrible guilt for having betrayed Dan who, while not exciting, had always been honest with her. She knew that she had broken a vow and as a consequence had permanently altered her own and many other people's lives. Her choice may have destroyed her husband's ability to trust again. Her parents no longer see Dan, even though they love him dearly.

Mary Lee did not delude herself that her actions were right, even at the time of the affair. But as many of us do when we transgress, she did delude herself in other ways. In her case as in many, the occlusion of the truth came in a quiet sequence: at first, she convinced herself that the affair would do no harm; next, she came to believe that it might result in something good. She told herself that the tenderness and acceptance she felt from the minister could possibly improve her relationship with her husband one day; finally, she came very close to feeling no guilt or sense of wrongdoing as the affair continued.

As most wrongdoers do, Mary Lee erected psychological defenses that allowed her to engage in unacceptable behavior. She found ways to justify her behavior to herself. However, she could not keep her defenses in place as her world began to come apart. People who must learn to forgive themselves are eventually unable to sustain the defense that convinced them of the benefits to their actions. Self-deception finally gives way to self-recrimination and guilt, which then prepares the way for the wrongdoer to begin the process of self-forgiveness.

More About Transgressions

Transgressions are generally considered to be actions taken by one person that interfere with another person's life course or plan. This interference puts the other person at a disadvantage, and is, at the same time, unauthorized. Transgressors are not given permission to do wrong. The confusing thing about transgressions is that what constitutes a wrongdoing is a relative notion. Sometimes an activity may be wrong, while at other times, the same activity may be right. Lying, stealing, killing, or breaking promises are all considered to be morally wrong sometimes, yet honorable at other times. This is one reason that philosophers debate wrongdoing and the average person is befuddled by it.

For example, a man might be thought of as considerate if he lies to a friend that he looks good in spite of a terminal illness, but if the man lies to his boss about a job not completed, he would be considered wrong. A parent who steals cocaine from his daughter's bedroom to protect her, would, in some people's opinion, not be considered wrong. Some philosophers have argued that lying, killing, cheating, or promise-breaking are always wrong regardless of their outcomes; whereas others argue that these activities are judged as right or wrong based on the outcomes they bring.* Although philosophers have debated the nature of right and wrong for centuries, the average person can only pick his way through the myriad of moral choices and try, as best he can, to make correct decisions.

When a person feels the need to forgive herself for wrongdoings, she, at least, has come to the conclusion that her actions were not morally neutral. We usually become aware of whether our behavior is perceived by others as neutral or wrong through the reaction of friends and family members. Dan's friends all think Mary Lee was wrong, no matter how unhappy she may have been. They think that she should have talked with Dan about her unhappiness rather than engaging in an illicit affair. Mary Lee's family members, too, believe that she was wrong.

Transgressions have some of the same characteristics of personal limitations. Both reveal previously hidden aspects of a person's makeup to the offended person and the community, and both result in injury that cannot be undone simply by an apology. The exposed part of the injurer,

---

*Ethical absolutists, known as *deontologists*, believe in the overriding importance of fixed moral rules. Actions are inherently right or wrong. Ethical relativists, known as *teleologists*, believe that an action is right or wrong depending on its consequences. The most influential absolutist was Immanuel Kant. Among influential relativists are Jeremy Bentham and, perhaps, Grotius and Thomas Aquinas.

however, does not necessarily reveal a flaw in character. Instead, it reveals a plan, and that plan exposes what that person covets or values. Mary Lee wanted comfort and intimacy. Thieves want money. Liars want power. When you do something that injures others, you reveal your hidden desires and how far you will go to meet them.

Mary Lee planned her affair carefully. She decided where it would occur and how often. She even planned its duration, telling herself from the outset that she would end it in a year. More important, Mary Lee planned to continue the affair until it was sure to benefit her one way or another. If it did not improve her marriage, she had planned to use Reverend Smith as her "transition relationship" out of the marriage. Once she felt strong enough, she believed she would be in a better position to make further choices about her future.

Mary Lee's plan revealed how self-consumed she really was and how her values were oriented to her own well-being, despite the potential harm to anyone else that her actions might cause. Like most of us, she cloaked herself in rationalization until too much damage occurred.

Mary Lee rationalized that the love she received from Reverend Smith could only improve her as a person, even at the cost of her marriage. She believed that because she had been raised in a home with little overt affection, she had not learned how to communicate her feelings. She had seen the disappointment in her husband's eyes during times of intimacy. And although she was bored with him, she was also self-searching enough to wonder if her limitations with intimacy and affection had driven him into gardening and TV watching. Mary Lee may indeed have been a victim, as is the case with people who have been inappropriately seduced by a manipulative professional; but Mary Lee knows in her heart that she still made certain choices, and that many of them were wrong.

Most wrongdoers, except those with evil intent, violate their moral agreements without intending to harm others. In fact, most wrongdoers probably hope that their transgressions will not ever be found out. Like Mary Lee, Karen also hoped to carry out a plan without being detected.

Karen asked Kim, her sister, if she could borrow one of Kim's favorite evening dresses. She told Kim she had to attend a business dinner dance because she knew her sister would not lend her the dress if she knew where Karen really intended to wear it.

Kim's marriage had dissolved two years earlier in a bitter battle over child custody. Having been granted half-time custody, Kim loathes her ex-husband and expects her family members to have nothing to do with him or his family. But her ex-husband was hosting a huge political bash, and Karen intended to wear the dress to the party, hoping to impress a man in whom she was very interested. Without knowing this, Kim lent Karen the dress.

A few days after the party, Kim's work associate told her how surprised she was to see Karen at the party, considering the host was Kim's ex-husband. When Kim asked her friend to describe Karen's dress, she became irate. Kim told Karen she never wanted to see her again. The betrayal permanently damaged the sisters' relationship.

Karen—like all wrongdoers who must learn to forgive themselves—breached the moral standards of her relationship with her sister for personal gain. She wanted to go to the party. She wanted to look pretty and be noticed. Her best chance at achieving these ends, she felt, meant borrowing Kim's dress and wearing it to Kim's ex-husband's home. The gains, she felt, seemed to outweigh the damage her deception would wreak.

Moral histories between two people become more and more complex as people mature together through ordinary times and crises. A couple may redefine their ideas of right and wrong when they consider how to help a troubled child, when they must make decisions about how to spend their money, or when they must care for a sick parent. Karen and Kim both knew how the other felt about deception. In the realm of their shared moral history, deception had been ruled out as intolerable in their relationship. Similarly, Mary Lee knew full well her husband's feelings about affairs. They had discussed infidelity numerous times when they discussed films and plays, their parents' marriages, and the divorces of friends. Mary Lee knew that Dan considered adultery as the ultimate betrayal, but she chose to go ahead with her relationship with Reverend Smith anyway—not with the intent to hurt her husband, but to "grow" as a person.

When people violate legal, religious, and personal moral agreements with no intent to harm, there are usually two common motives:

1. Wrongdoers intend that the wrongdoing will result in the acquisition of desired objects, events, or achievements.
2. Wrongdoers believe that their transgressions will result in something valued not being taken from them.

Things desired might be material or non-material. People may want to acquire cars, jewelry, or drugs; or they may desire an increase in status, reputation, popularity, or power. Conversely, most people are reluctant to lose power, money, prestige, status, love, or material things and may go to great lengths to preserve them. Transgressors cross moral boundaries to maintain ownership of the things they value. The characteristics of transgressions are, then, that they violate moral codes, that they are intentional, that they are not intended to harm, and that they are carried out for personal gain. The characteristics of transgressions do not apply to false transgressions.

FALSE TRANSGRESSIONS

Many people feel bad about themselves because they very often believe that they have done something wrong, particularly in relation to a specific person. Sometimes these people are sure of what these "wrongdoings" are; sometimes they are not. False transgressions and the guilt and pain that accompany them can be crippling; and people who try to "forgive" themselves for them are stymied because the need for forgiveness is false also. Where there are false wrongdoings, there is nothing to be forgiven for and nothing to forgive oneself for. Michael felt "wrong" most of his life, and when "self-forgiveness" would not come, he sought counseling.

~≈≈~

Michael could not forgive himself when his mother died just prior to his twenty-eighth birthday. He felt as though he had betrayed her. Michael had finally moved out of her home when he was twenty-seven. He had begun to date a very nice woman and was living happily on his own when his mother found she had ovarian cancer.

With his therapist, Michael traced the history of his guilt and perpetual belief that he had done something wrong. As a boy, he remembered how much his mother loved her show dogs. He recalled that sometimes she would leave him alone for the weekend to go to dog shows, telling him there was not enough room in the car for him and the dogs. He recalled a time when money was scarce, and he and his mother ate hot dogs while the dogs continued to be fed the highest-quality dog food available.

Remembering always feeling guilty, the young man recalled a compulsion to apologize to his mother that began when he was nine or ten years old. He remembered clearly her angry scolding of him when he asked why he should go to church. He also remembered feeling ashamed in public because he felt he was not good enough to be seen with her.

At seventeen, Michael was accepted at a fine university. His mother reacted by further attacking his self-worth. She repeatedly and harshly admonished him that no decent son abandons his mother, even for an excellent education. Michael

*abandoned his plans for college and stayed at home. He
believed that, by doing so, he was meeting his moral obligations as a son; yet he began to feel even more depressed and
guilt-ridden. When he finally developed enough strength and
maturity, at twenty-seven, to leave home, he was dogged by
the sense that moving out of his mother's home was, indeed, a
moral failing. This sense heightened when, before she finally
died, his mother relentlessly skewered him with accusations of
his wrongdoings. Unable to bear her spite and not knowing how
to seek support from his woman friend, he ended their friendship and retreated into silent guilt. Michael believed he had
transgressed his moral relationship with his mother, when,
actually, he had done nothing wrong.*

False transgressions show some of the same characteristics as false limitations. Just as false limitations are not obvious to "outsiders," false
transgressions are not obvious to others because no wrongdoing has
occurred. False wrongdoings, like false limitations, are defined by only
one person in a relationship, not both. One person begins to dictate the
moral terms of the relationship instead of negotiating them together.
In addition, where false wrongdoings are perceived, the following
may occur:

1. There may be appear to be agreement between the two as to what
   is right and wrong, but the agreement on one person's part is not
   freely given.
2. There may be compliance to an accepted the moral contract, but the
   compliance is a product of guilt, self-doubt, or fear rather than one of
   healthy agreement.

Michael never freely agreed to his mother's understanding about
what was required of dutiful children. He knew that total attention and

absolute loyalty were what his mother demanded of him. He had felt the weight of guilt when he was unable to live up to her unrealistic standard. He also saw other men his age with wives and families, and being a person of some strength, he had managed to break free of her. In addition, he had begun to rewrite his contract with her, attempting to introduce some of his own moral terms. She had strictly defined her requirements of him, but he had had no power to define his requirements of her as a mother. He had begun the process of renegotiating the terms of his relationship with her when his mother died.

In a true moral law between people, there is "mutual voluntary allegiance of both persons to a principle."[19] This allegiance is not coerced, and the principle is mutually defined by both parties. Michael's mother's principle of loyalty, at least as it applied to her son, meant total commitment without interruption, interference, or competition. Her ideas of loyalty were completely one-sided and did not take into consideration the basic rights and needs of her son. Michael's ideas of loyalty were broader and more flexible. He felt he could be loyal to more than one person at a time and, on some level, he recognized that his mother was more loyal to her dogs than her son. With the help of friends and his counselor, he came to understand that his concept of loyalty was as legitimate as his mother's, and, perhaps, more so. He began to see that he had done nothing wrong, but instead had been shamed into compliance with the terms of a moral contract with which he did not agree. Although he still grieved his mother's death, he determined that he had treated her well and had nothing to forgive himself for. Michael was able to go on with his life as a much happier person, unburdened by his false sense of having failed as a son.

Interpersonal moral agreements are mutually written and continue to change over time when people encounter new moral challenges. Legal and religious codes, by contrast, are less likely to change—especially written religious proscriptions and codes of conduct. Is it possible for a person to feel wrong—when he actually is not—in relation to an unchanging written legal or religious proscription? This was Linda's situation.

Linda believed in daily contemplative prayer. She believed it was wrong not to pray. She also believed that a good person who prayed with the correct spiritual attitude would have her prayers answered. Since her youth, she had relied on a special scripture to show her whether she was morally on-course or not—Matthew 7:7: "Ask, and it shall be given you; seek, and ye shall find; knock, and it shall be opened unto you." Linda used this text as a moral barometer, always checking her moral conduct against this mandate. The verse had proved to be almost magical, because when she seemed to be in the right moral frame of mind, she always received what she asked for. When she did not, she believed her faith was not strong enough, probably because of some action or unrecognized thoughts that had displeased God.

When Linda's teenage son was arrested for drug trafficking, Linda prayed for his acquittal. When he was convicted, she prayed that the next court would overturn the conviction. When he was sent to prison, she prayed for an early parole. Linda asked and asked, but when her prayers were not answered, she concluded that she must have done something very wrong or else God would have answered her prayers.

Linda could not "forgive" herself for failing her son and God at such a critical time; but her sense of wrongdoing was as false as Michael's. Her belief in the scripture was not coerced, but it was proved to be a false and limiting belief. Linda could not see that simply believing a religious prescript so fervently could not control her son's behavior or other events in her life. And although she was convinced she had done something "wrong," her friends could see no reason for her self-recrimination.

Linda had never considered how other people interpreted scripture, but feeling as bad about herself as she did, she finally sought help from her minister. He immediately set about helping her find relief from her increasing, unwarranted sense of guilt. The minister interpreted the scripture differently from Linda, and in his view, there was no direct causal relationship between not receiving answers to her prayers and wrong spiritedness. He helped Linda see that the answers to prayers may come at a later time or in a different form than expected. He helped her to recognize that her literal interpretation of the scripture was not only guilt-inducing, but was faulty.

For some people, self-blame becomes a part of their character.[20] This may be especially true of people who have been inaccurately, but routinely blamed by parents or marriage partners. A husband constantly blamed by his wife for violating her expectations may come to think less of himself until his self-esteem is so eroded that self-blame is habitual. If people recall that actual wrongdoings are committed for personal gain, they can then assess whether they have really done something wrong or are being falsely criticized for *someone else's* benefit. The husband who blames himself for his wife's unhappiness has gained no benefits from her unhappiness; but her "unhappiness" has directly benefited her because she has used it to make her husband feel obligated to her.

꒦꒷

Charmayne, like Michael, felt guilty and obligated. Her husband used her sense of obligation to control her. In her case, though, Charmayne recognized early on that hers was a false transgression and used the recognition to improve her marriage.

Charmayne was accused again of serving a terrible meal. Again, her husband was angry. Again, she felt guilty and bad. Charmayne's husband accused her of violating the marital principle that she should love and honor him. If she loved him, he said, she would cook him decent meals. Her husband gained more and more power over her through his demands and her increasing self-loathing. Finally, she realized that the moral law was being defined by her husband alone. She did not agree that love and honor were synonymous with good food. Nor did

she agree that love and honor were compatible with being
berated by one's partner. Charmayne's friends agreed with her.
So did her therapist and minister.

Charmayne demanded that her husband go to marriage
counseling with her to discuss their expectations of each other
and what expectations were negotiable and non-negotiable.
After months of discussion, a reasonable agreement was
hammered out, and Charmayne's marriage was back on
course. This time both parties agreed as to what was wrong or
not wrong and both were freely willing to comply with
the agreement.

꩜

TRANSGRESSIONS AND SELF-JUSTIFICATION

Actual transgressions cross over a boundary that destroys the trust of
another person. The wronged party sees clearly that the other person
took an independent course during which she either changed her own
ideas or engaged in wrongdoings despite her professed allegiance to a
specific moral contract. In the wake of wrongdoing is broken trust. If
trust in the relationship is to be regained, it will likely come as a result of
the wrongdoer recognizing and admitting to the wrongdoing.

Yet wrongdoers almost always justify their actions. Whether justifications stem from self-delusion—like Mary Lee's—or are elaborate
rationalizations, justifications attempt to place transgressions in some logical and meaningful context within the moral agreement between the
people involved. Tim's attempt at justifying having broken a promise to
his best friend, Nolan, is a good example.

꩜

Tim asked Nolan if he could borrow Nolan's second car for a
couple of days while his was in the repair shop. Nolan knew
that Tim was sometimes irresponsible, but when Tim nearly

begged him and gave his word that he would take care of the car and return it promptly, Nolan lent him the car. A week later, the car had not been returned.

Nolan tried to reach Tim at home. The machine was not on. At work, no one had seen him. Then Nolan got worried that Tim had had an accident. He called the police, but no accident had been reported.

Over the next two days, Nolan became furious. When Tim pulled into the driveway ten days after borrowing the car, Nolan was ready to end their friendship on the spot. But Tim, on seeing Nolan, put up his hands and spoke:

"I know you're angry with me, but hear me out. After I got your car to my house, the phone rang, and it was Grandmother Shaw. You know her. She said that Grandfather had had a mild stroke and was terribly combative. She begged me to come immediately and not tell anyone. I tried to call you, despite her request, but you were nowhere to be found. So for the past ten days, I've been struggling with a physically violent old man, a broken-hearted and frightened old woman, lawyers, nursing home administrators, and hysterical family members. I'll pay for the use of your car, like I would have paid a rental company. I could use a drink, old friend. Can I come in?"

Nolan gave in, despite vague feelings of being taken advantage of, and let Tim in.

Justifications take three forms in addition to the ubiquitous claim that no harm was intended. They are:

1. A higher good will result from breaking the moral agreement. The wrongdoer truly believes that the betrayed person will also agree that the higher good was more important than their agreement.

2. Another moral agreement overrode the one between the wrongdoer and the person betrayed.
3. The relationship had never encountered an event that challenged its basic moral terms. Having no time to discuss the impact such an action would have on the relationship, the wrongdoer simply acted. Unhappily, this action damaged the relationship.

Some people attempt to use all these justifications; some only one. Mary Lee tried to use two of them to restore her relationship with Dan to its previous moral terms.

Dan was inconsolable. Mary Lee told him at first that she believed the good that came from the affair would help their marriage. The Reverend Smith had really meant little to her, she reasoned. When her husband didn't respond, she tried to tell him that she had been so taken aback by Reverend Smith's advances she didn't know what to do. She reasoned with him that she had been so shocked and confused that she gave in to the seduction. This, too, did not restore her husband's faith in her.

Justifications are used in an attempt to convince the injured that actions taken were morally acceptable. Excuses, by contrast, are used to convince people that behavior may not have been right, but should be viewed as being blameless. The most common excuses used by wrongdoers are that they were, somehow, "not themselves." They were temporarily disabled by being distraught, confused, ill, or under the influence of a mood-altering substance.

Mary Lee tried to convince her husband she was not to blame. She was nothing more than a victim, she argued. She had fallen under the power of a predator who had used her vulnerability for his own pleasure.

Finally, she told her husband that some good was already coming about as a result of her indiscretion: they were really talking once again and finally being honest with each other.

Tim used the second justification and no excuses. He explained to Nolan that he was unexpectedly faced with a moral duty that was at least as important as his promise to Nolan. He had to make a quick decision, and he chose his duty to his grandparents. He said he hoped that Nolan, being a reasonable man, would see his dilemma and, even if grudgingly, accept his choice.

Beth, too, chose the second justification.

⤞⥝

Beth, sixteen, knew that her mother loathed deceit in any form. So did Beth. At the mall one day, Beth saw her mother's boyfriend with another woman. Soon after, her mother confided in Beth that she was worried her boyfriend was drifting away from her. She asked Beth directly if she knew of any reason that might be true. Beth said no. Later, when the boyfriend walked out, Beth told her mother about the other woman. Beth's mother was furious, but when Beth explained that she had hidden the truth to protect her mother's feelings, the woman understood. They revisited their agreement to always tell the truth, though, and Beth's mother said that she would like to be told the truth no matter how painful it may be. Beth agreed, and the two were able to begin to trust each other again.

⤞⥝

Beth's wrongdoing did not permanently harm her relationship because she had tried to take her mother's feelings into consideration when she lied. Mary Lee, however, was unable to successfully and reasonably justify her actions, and her husband left her. And even Nolan, although sympathetic to Tim's dilemma, decided that justification alone would not repair the damage done to their relationship. He decided he could no longer trust Tim and ended their friendship. Both Mary Lee and Tim, their relationships permanently damaged, will experience the full pain of their transgressions. Mary Lee, Tim, and others whose wrongdoing cannot be undone must now cope with the deeper meanings of their breaches.

When people break laws or moral obligations, the facades they have erected in their private lives also are broken down. When people try to forgive themselves, the self-delusion ends. Some "wrong" behavior has little impact on the wrongdoer even if it results in injury to others. These people do not concern themselves with self-forgiveness because their intent is to increase personal gain no matter what. People who struggle with forgiveness are those who have intact consciences, but who, at one time, distanced themselves from really seeing what they truly value.

Since Dan's departure, Mary Lee has become painfully aware of her wrongdoing and has begun to honestly view herself. For the first time in her life, she is acknowledging the fact that she has always lied when it suited her. She is also aware that she has a tendency to seek the attention and approval of people she believes to be important and powerful. She is having trouble telling people she was bored with her husband. She knows, in reality, that he had not risen in professional or social circles as she had hoped. Mary Lee is beginning to realize that she valued being "special" to someone she thought to be influential more than she valued being honest in her marriage. She also recognizes that being special has always been key to her self-concept, so much so that in the past, she lied and cheated to promote her uniqueness. For the first time she is aware that some of her friends have been talking about her in disparaging ways, and for the first time, her facade has been so lifted that she clearly sees herself. She has lost most of what meant something to her because of her narcissism. For this, she will try to forgive herself.

The Reverend Smith must also try to forgive himself. He has always recognized his insatiable appetite for power over people; his charm and charisma worked for him in the pulpit, and his political savvy worked as he moved up through the church ranks. During that rise, he had begun to see himself as a man with almost limitless potential. His affair with Mary Lee was not his first sexual relationship with a parishioner; but it would be his last. Even if the trust of his parishioners and his church cannot be repaired, he is determined to confront his wrongdoings, own them, isolate his flaws, and, hopefully, one day, forgive himself.

Apologies

Reverend Smith apologized to his congregation for breaking their trust. His apology was taken by almost everyone as a self-serving attempt to regain his power. The congregation did not trust him; his apology could not undo the harm of his actions.

Mary Lee apologized to Dan's parents. They were gracious and accepting of her because they had loved her; but their relationship with her will never be the same, even though they have known her since she was a young girl.

People who have willfully violated the trust of their loved ones will often find their apologies go unaccepted. This does not preclude them, however, from learning from their mistakes. They may find that self-forgiveness may be required without the forgiveness of others.

Confronting the Self-as-Feared

Mary Lee remembered in a divorce recovery group that once in high school, she had caused the break-up of a much-admired relationship between two of her classmates. She had gotten drunk and had sex with the boy. Everyone in her class found out about it, but over the years, she had "forgotten" about it. She had distanced herself from this incident and many others wherein she had injured others, so that she had come to live as something of an impostor. Now she was beginning to see how she had lived in denial of her actions, and the experience of gaining self-knowledge was often uncomfortable and painful.

After Tim lost Nolan's friendship, he began to see things about himself that he had managed to deny. A social worker by profession, his public persona was that of a charitable man who drove an older car, camped out when he traveled, eschewed wealth, and "walked what he talked." He knows, as does Nolan, that under all the verbiage is an envious man who resents not having the "good life" of more wealthy professional men. Like Mary Lee, he is facing his self-as-feared, and he does not like what he sees.

For Mary Lee, Tim, and others who will try to forgive themselves, an honest confrontation with the unacceptable and avoided parts of self will be a large part of self-forgiveness. This confrontation is not pleasurable, though, and requires a level of courage that many of us do not have.

Mary Lee has lost faith in most of the beliefs she had held dear. She believed in the church and had faith that those close to God would not use other people to their own advantage. She also had believed that God would always guide her to make wise decisions; now she was unsure of God's role in the loss of her marriage. She had trusted her own judgment and had believed that people who get into messes and damage their lives deserve what they get. She believes that she had tried to be a good person for most of her life, but that somewhere, something went wrong. More difficult, Mary Lee had thought that Dan would be with her through "thick and thin" and that, as a man of his word, he would not violate his marriage vows even when she had. Many of her basic assumptions had been shattered with the end of her marriage. She would now have to work hard—and courageously—to learn from her mistakes.

Wrongdoers who engage in the process of self-discovery also gain new perspectives on other people. They can no longer assume that other people will accept their actions. Wrongdoers learn that they have lost the false sense of control they believed they held over others.

People who transgress might also wonder about the benevolence of others. If a person commits a crime and goes to jail, he may no longer be able to assume that he will be trusted by others even after he has paid his debt. Punishment, either by society or by an individual, might not really "clean the slate" so that a wrongdoer cannot simply assume that the world will remain benevolent and trusting. With the process of self-forgiveness, however, comes the opportunity to replace our assumptions about ourselves and the world around us, and rebuild a more realistic, healthy, and honest moral sense of ourselves.

Summary

Mary Lee feels as if she has been shut out of the important things in her life. She begged Dan to go to therapy with her, but he refused. He has permanently rejected her. She feels on the outside of her friendship circles and family, and even worse, she does not know how to gain reentry. For Mary Lee to forgive herself, she will have to build roads back to other people, this time with honesty. She will need to accept the fact that she broke promises to people all her life when it served her needs. She will have to look closely at her values and not deny that the affair that ruined her marriage was tied to them. She will have to try to repair relationships when and if she can. Whether she is never forgiven by her family and friends, or if all forgive her, is irrelevant if she does not begin to understand herself better and make some profound personal changes.

When people breach the core contracts of their moral lives, whether they inadvertently risk harm or intend harm, key aspects of their lives are damaged. Gone is the cavalier notion that one can do what one knows to be wrong and suffer no repercussions. Gone is the false idea that people will not hold them accountable, blame them, and even leave them.

A person who lies, cheats, breaks promises, abuses, physically injures, or murders to achieve some sort of personal gain is rendered transparent to loved ones or the broader community. Her true values shine in the glare of discovery. From this place Mary Lee and all wrongdoers must start the process of self-forgiveness.

CHAPTER 4

Wrongdoings That Kill

Kurt decided it was time to drive home and got up from the bar stool. His Blazer was right outside the door as usual. The road home was all that stood between him and a cold supper. Over the course of that hot summer afternoon, sounds of the slot machines, clinking ice, muffled voices, and the music from the jukebox flooded together to form familiar relief from the scorching heat. Even the neon-lighted waterfall on the Coors ad above the bar seemed to cool the place. Kurt was drunk, and he felt powerful and happy. As he rose to leave, everybody in the bar knew not to protest. Kurt could be mean, and he never allowed anyone to take his keys. The popular young man laid some bills out on the bar, walked to the parking lot, stepped up into his Blazer, and pulled onto the country road. The route to his house took him through one small town, onto a four-lane highway for several miles, and then off onto a stretch of rolling road.

Once he was off the four-lane and on the final leg of his trip home, he cranked up Vince Gill on his radio and acceler-ated to seventy-five miles an hour. He had not known that for the entire drive, he had been weaving badly between the center line and the right apron of the road. When he reached the third hill, about a mile from his house, he floored the accelerator to eighty, and when he did, the right front wheel fell off the roadway into a ditch. He panicked. He spun the steering wheel to the left as hard as he could, careening to the other side of the road. He struck a car with four popular teenagers in it. The driver was killed instantly; the front seat passenger sustained severe head injuries; and the other two suffered multiple cuts and breaks. Kurt was arrested. His blood alcohol level was .22, far above the legal limit. He was charged with homicide by reckless use of a vehicle.

The entire community was devastated. Some called for life in prison for Kurt. Others pleaded for mercy for him. It was not so long ago that he had been one of the most talented football players ever to play at the local high school. Most people also knew that Kurt's father had committed suicide. He, too, had been a problem drinker. At the trial, his mother pleaded for mercy, but Kurt was found guilty of manslaughter and was incarcerated. He will be eligible for parole in another four years.

☙❧

What is it about Kurt's case that is likely to trouble more people than a case like Jonas's or Katherine's? What might people say when asked if Kurt deserves a chance to forgive himself? Do we think that Kurt deserves less of a chance to repair his life because he took a life? Are we so disapproving that we believe a drunk person has no right to forgiveness?

No doubt in our society many people vilify drivers who drink. Even more detest drunk drivers who take lives. Do drunk drivers have any less "right" to forgive themselves than income tax evaders, unfaithful spouses, or those who commit more mundane acts of wrongdoing? Should Kurt be encouraged to forgive himself, and should we try to forgive him; or do some of us deserve forgiveness or the "right" to forgive ourselves more than others?

Kurt wants to work toward forgiveness. He feels much remorse and guilt. He has struggled to make amends to the parents who lost their child. He has offered to pay for therapy for the grieving family, even if it takes him the rest of his life. He wrote open letters to the community, admitting his drinking problem. He has sworn he will never drink again. And he has sat in his jail cell, truly trying to understand and change his behavior. Some people in the community have expressed a willingness to accept him; others have not. Now, he believes that if he is to ever function again as a reasonably contributing member of society, he has to forgive himself. Otherwise, he will remain stuck in the role of wrongdoer and will be unable to make any further contributions to life. Is Kurt that different from the rest of us?

Kurt was wrong when he decided to drive home drunk that evening. He broke a law against driving under the influence of alcohol. Like Mary Lee, he did not violate a law or rule with the intent of hurting someone else. Instead, like all of us who break agreements that require forgiveness, he did so to benefit himself. Kurt drove under the influence because he enjoyed the "buzz" and euphoria of driving fast while intoxicated. He, like most people trying to forgive themselves, intended no harm, but caused great pain to others. The great difference is that Kurt's wrongdoing ended in someone else's death. If manslaughter or murder negates the chance for finding forgiveness, then it would be true that soldiers who kill on the battlefield or doctors whose knives slip during surgery would also lose their right to forgiveness. Kurt loathes himself. Like Katherine, Mary Lee, and Jonas, he hates himself for what he did to others and for what he let his life become. Like all of us who want to be forgiven by the people we hurt, Kurt feels deep self-recrimination for what he did. He no longer can deny his drinking problem and is poised to change his life.

Since the "accident," Kurt has thought often about his inability to listen to people who tried to help him in the past. He is aware of his arrogance and bad judgment. He remembers many mornings when he woke up so hungover he could barely walk. He recalls being abusive, once even hitting a girl he dated in high school. He remembers having vomited on the wall of his kitchen one night after drinking a case of beer and a half-pint of gin. He remembers verbally attacking his former best friend, who had tried to help him stop drinking. He remembers waking up with women he did not know and being unable to eat for days due to nausea. Kurt may have been blind to himself, as all of us are to some degree, but he is blind no longer.

Kurt knows that he is helpless to bring back the young person he killed. He knows he cannot change the fact that he got in his car and drove drunk. He is exposed and ashamed and feels helpless to change anything. This is when the process of growth and self-forgiveness can begin.

In a very real sense, self-forgiveness is the act of taking control. It hinges on action. The process of self-forgiveness allows people to take charge of their lives again. We may be helpless to change the past, but we are not helpless to change the future. This is the conclusion that Kurt and the others have all drawn. They want to take action and release themselves from self-hatred so that their lives can go on.

Some people may believe that Kurt and others have no "right" to forgive themselves because they have not learned a lesson. This is certainly not true for Kurt. He has much more to learn about himself, to be sure, but this will happen if he attempts the process of self-forgiveness. He has already learned, sadly, that many people in his community were not what he thought; neighbors, and even former teachers, called for the death penalty in his case. Hardly a day went by during his first year in jail that he did not receive hate mail. Old friends do not call or visit. He is, profoundly, alone.

Before the accident, Kurt did not have an accurate perception of himself, and this gross misperception was reinforced by others in his life. His view of himself did not spring from a vacuum. Other people "helped" him develop and maintain it.

Take, for instance, Kurt's high school football coach. Coach Daniels was a respected community leader, county board member, and family man. He understood that Kurt's own dad had had many personal problems, so he took Kurt "under his wing"—not because he was altruistic, but because he needed a good football player to win games for him. Kurt was a good athlete and Coach Daniels wanted to use him. Early in this relationship, Coach Daniels began to teach Kurt that he was different, special. If Kurt did not do his homework, Coach made it a point to talk to the teachers. If Kurt failed a test, Coach negotiated so that he could retake it. Unlike the other boys, when Kurt felt lazy, he was not required to run laps or do pushups. Coach Daniels reinforced the idea that Kurt could break rules and get away with it. The first time Kurt came to a game drunk, Coach Daniels needed him that night, so he let him play. Soon the boy's drinking before and after games became a common and accepted occurrence.

Kurt began to believe that he did not have to obey rules or laws. At the same time, Kurt's mother, herself troubled, began to rely on Kurt to be "the man of the house." She relied on him to help make everyday decisions. Eventually, she relied on him to take responsibility for their dysfunctional household. When her husband fell asleep drunk, she asked Kurt to put him to bed. When his father died, Kurt bore the casket, comforted his mother, and gave the eulogy. Then he got drunk. Girls in town loved the strapping athlete, and boys valued his companionship and great humor. No one in his community intervened or expressed any concern over the inordinate demands placed on him at home or the unrestricted leniency allowed him at school. In his town, every public event was celebrated with alcohol. Whether at the Memorial Day parade, a summer picnic, or a fall football game, people drank with abandon. Jokes about drinking were commonplace. In fact, when Kurt was first stopped for drinking by the county sheriff, the sheriff just winked. Later, as community pressures against drunk driving grew, Kurt was finally picked up; but he was never punished for it. In fact, the community joked about his drinking problem.

Like all of us, Kurt lived with illusions about himself. Until he killed someone, he saw himself as a wild, crazy, fun-loving, risk-taking, rule-breaking, popular man. Kurt is not all that different from other people who seek self-forgiveness. He killed someone, but others ruin people's trust, strip them of faith in a parent's love, or permanently damage their capacity to believe in other people or relationships. There can be no doubt of the destructiveness of these kinds of injuries. The question remains: Does the severity of one type of injury preclude the right to self-forgiveness? And can we judge others as being unworthy of forgiveness when we may have contributed to their destructive lack of self-awareness?

Summary

Just as the worlds of the other people whose limitations, mistakes, and transgressions were described in earlier chapters, Kurt's world will have to be rebuilt, from the bottom up. His illusions of himself and violation of the law shattered his beliefs about his control over his life and his self-worth. Mary Lee's (Chapter 3) unwillingness to see herself accurately and her choice to transgress her marriage vows permanently altered her perception of herself, others, and God. Jonas (Chapter 2), whose "mistakes" were in reality character flaws, no longer feels in secure control of others or of his own capacity to manage people's impressions of him.

The worlds of all these people have come undone, and all face the challenge of self-forgiveness, like the one that you may face.

When you choose to forgive yourself, you have decided to be rid of hatred—self-hatred. You believe that hatred is defeating. You believe that you have lessons to learn and gifts to contribute to life. When you make the decision to forgive yourself, you commit yourself to being your own liberator, just as you commit yourself to liberating someone else when you forgive him. You are both the captive and liberator, and you must choose to free yourself from self-punishment and decide, instead, to make your way back to the human community. You have decided to discard your false assumptions and replace them with new, valid ones. You can do this alone, with friends, or with God's help. You can forgive yourself in a Veteran's Hospital being treated for post-traumatic stress disorder, in a prison where you pay your debt to society, or in a church when you are praying.

Kurt decided he had much to give back to life. He decided he wanted to join his community again, this time as himself, not some character born of self-delusion. He knew he had hard work to do, and he decided to do it. But he has decided to forgo interminable self-punishment for the sake of contributing whatever he can to the remainder of his life. Self-forgiveness is his only way back to others in his community, and he has chosen it. You, too, can make this choice.

PART II

Forgiving Yourself

SELF-FORGIVENESS is, in a very real sense, the smallest unit of peace-making. Wars are finalized between countries or tribes through the use of negotiation, diplomacy, and treaty-signing. Battles are ended between family members through the use of mediation, forbearance, forgetting, forgiveness, or simple resignation. Internal battles are ended, at least where peace is the result, through self-forgiveness.

At the end of any peacemaking effort, weapons will be put down, debts paid off, agreements made about people held in captivity, promises made, and further expectations established. It is the same with self-forgiveness. When people are able to forgive themselves, they accomplish the following:

1. They have become familiar with the "enemy within." They know how to keep it in check.
2. They have put away self-destructive emotional weapons, such as guilt and shame.
3. They have made promises to themselves and intend to keep them.
4. They look to the future free of the bad feelings associated with the injuries they brought about and the fear that they might injure, in

the same way, again. They describe themselves as "clean," "free," "lighter," and "happy again."

Self-forgiveness does not come about easily, though. It can take years to accomplish, if there is no help or if a person does not work very hard at it. Self-forgiveness also does not necessarily erase regret. A person might always wish that some other outcome had happened. Self-forgiveness does away with self-loathing and recrimination, but it does not erase the past.

When we forgive ourselves, we make peace with ourselves. We restore trust in ourselves. People who can forgive themselves ordinarily come to see themselves more realistically than they once did. They are more comfortable with themselves, flaws and all.

How do people accomplish self-forgiveness; and what barriers do they face? The second part of this book addresses these two questions and provides concrete suggestions for people who would like to be free from self-hatred. It should be stated at the outset of Part II, though, that self-forgiveness is one of the most difficult processes a person can face.

To forgive other people, you can make excuses for them or pretend they meant no harm. Injured people can second-guess their injurers and tell themselves that an injurer was a victim of circumstances, or ill, or drunk, perhaps. Empathy, self-deception, and compassion can lead the way to forgiving another person. Where your self is concerned, though, excuses are much more difficult to mount. A person knows his or her own intentions, mean-spiritedness, or limitations much better than other people do. When one person damages another or ruins a relationship, he alone knows what lay in his heart at the time. For this reason, many people have less tolerance for their own mistakes than for other people's. People know themselves all too well to simply excuse their mistakes— especially when those mistakes have brought about interpersonal ruin.

Self-forgiveness results from the desire to face yourself as honestly as possible and come to terms with any personal flaws that might injure others. It is the clearing away of excuses and myths about yourself. Therefore, self-forgiveness is humbling. But people who accomplish it agree that it is worth the effort, because at the end, you can go on with life free of the burdens of self-loathing and guilt.

There are four phases of self-forgiveness. Each is described in a following chapter and accompanied with exercises to help you move through each phase. The word "phase" is used here to help readers organize concepts. It is not meant as a scientific, or maturational, concept that implies an inviolable sequential ordering of phenomena, one falling before or after another in a specific, predictable order. "Phase" is used as an overarching idea that gives guidance to people who are attempting to forgive themselves so that they can see the "big picture" and any tasks that need to be accomplished to make self-forgiveness complete.

The four phases of self-forgiveness are as follows:

1. Phase 1: Confronting Yourself
2. Phase 2: Holding Yourself Responsible
3. Phase 3: Confessing Your Flaws
4. Phase 4: Transformation

Accomplishing each phase is important to free yourself from self-imposed captivity. To engage in them, though, you will need to believe that your life ahead is worth the hard work of self-forgiveness. In other words, you must want to forgive yourself more than you want to be held captive to non-forgiveness. For some people, self-forgiveness is accomplished through hard work alone. For others, professional therapy aids the process. For still others, God's grace is the key to forgiveness and self-forgiveness alike. No one approach is right for everyone; people struggling to forgive will want to choose the best combination of methods and the best sources of help to fit their situation and personal beliefs. However it is accomplished, freedom lies at the end of the struggle.

CHAPTER 5

Confronting Yourself

Candace had been raised to believe that she was unique. Her grandfather, a Baptist minister, and her grandmother, both widely recognized in their community, had taken her in when she was very young. They taught her about her special talents and obligations to the community. So when Candace got pregnant at eighteen, moved out, and refused to give the baby up for adoption, her grandparents rejected her. When they did, Candace decided to be easy on herself. She decided she had to be her own best friend if her grandparents would not come to her aid. After several months, although still hurt, the old couple took Candace and her baby back in, and all seemed well for a while. But soon after that, the young woman began to steal money from her trusting boss, Ted. Always in need of money but not entirely sure of the reasons she began to steal, Candace commenced to pilfer small sums from Ted's various accounts. Over a year's time, she took $3,500. Then the nightmares started, and Candace's days were filled with vague plans to pack up and leave town. Finally, the pressure was so intense that Candace admitted the thefts to Ted. Instead of prosecuting or even firing the young woman, Ted, who must have been a very *wise man, lent Candace the money to repay and reconcile the accounts. Instead of condemning her, he said to Candace, "I can live with this. Can you?" He never again spoke of the incident.*

Candace, through Ted's understanding attitude, had lost her outside enemy. She had no one but herself to blame or fight or condemn. For the first time in her life, Candace had to face herself. She began to recognize her own wrongness, greed, and arrogance. She came face-to-face with what she must forgive—not other people for their flaws—but herself, for her own shortcomings and failures.

The first phase of self-forgiveness, the one that Candace just began, is confronting yourself. Because self-forgiveness is a small form of peace-making, it is, as in any war, wise to understand the enemy. When you understand an enemy, it is easier to engage in negotiations toward ending hostilities.

The first phase of self-forgiveness is critical because *it is not possible to forgive yourself when you do not know what you are attempting to forgive.*

Candace would not have been able to forgive herself had she been allowed to blame Ted for firing her or punishing her in another way. Her own flaws and accountability would be lost in her anger at Ted. Ted would have been the enemy, not herself. False identification of what needs to be forgiven can delay or stall the process of self-forgiveness for a very long time; and delays in forgiving oneself can cause a lifetime of unnecessary self-delusion, cover-up, and pain.

Confronting yourself involves five steps:

1. Name any false limitation or wrongdoing you have labored under so that you can conclude whether you actually need to forgive yourself.
2. Identify the actual sources of the mistakes you have made.
3. Understand the fundamental assumptions about yourself that have been damaged and that you will need to repair.

4. Understand and identify your feelings about the incident you can't forgive.
5. Identify any barriers you might face when you try to see your own flaws or mistakes more realistically.

Candace must look at herself in a new and naked light. To forgive, the light of self-discovery and self-understanding must shine brightly on the one who is to be forgiven, whether a person concludes it is herself or someone else.

Step 1: Name false limitations and false wrongdoings

The first step of self-forgiveness requires an injurer to thoroughly examine the accuracy of her assessment of personal limitations or wrongdoings. A person cannot "forgive" herself if there is nothing to forgive.

Chapters 2 and 3 described the characteristics of false limitations and wrongdoings. When you take the first step in the process of self-forgiveness, you will assess these characteristics. Then you can clarify whether you are accountable for harming someone or something, or whether your flaws or mistakes have caused no harm at all.

The characteristics of false limitations or wrongdoings are, again, as follows:

> False limitations and wrongdoings are defined as harmful by others and are not merely recognized and felt emotionally by the person who has perpetrated the presumed injury. Both are used by others to manipulate people into compliance with their own personal agendas. People who believe they have broken their moral contracts with others may have had no part in negotiating the terms of those contracts. Instead, they may have complied with the terms only because they were punished or shamed when they did not.

When a person who has not actually wounded someone as a result of her limitations, mistakes, or wrongdoings tells others that she is responsible for ruining relationships or causing harm, these other people simply cannot agree that she, alone, is responsible for the harm.

In the first step of self-forgiveness, a person will ask herself a series of questions:

1. Was I the first person to know that my limitation or wrongdoing hurt someone? If the people I hurt knew, did they use the experience against me to make me feel pain?
2. Have the people who said I hurt them or whom I actually hurt recounted this repeatedly, even if I am not sure that I did something wrong?
3. Has my guilt or shame increased over time, primarily because another person continues to condemn me and not because my self-searching reveals things I do not like about myself?
4. Are the "victims" of my mistake profiting in any way at my expense? Are they receiving attention, or gaining power over me?

In Chapter 3, Michael, whose mother in essence held him captive, would have answered "yes" to all these questions. So would Marietta, whose husband blamed his affairs on her cooking and weight. When you take the first step of self-forgiveness, check to see if you have a history of feeling guilty or ashamed around the person you supposedly harmed. You may be feeling these things again but have done nothing that needs to be forgiven. The emotions you may be experiencing are simply familiar, so you might wrongly conclude, as Michael did when his mother died, that once again, you are wrong. When guilt and shame become familiar companions, inaccurate self-blame can frequently follow.

Forgiving yourself starts with a process of elimination. In the first step, you thoughtfully and carefully examine the event in your life for which you believe you need to be forgiven by asking yourself the preceding four questions. If you find something about yourself that you must forgive, then you move forward into the remainder of the process. If, on the other hand, you find that your faults, mistakes, and limitations are being used by others to manipulate you and that they are partly, but most certainly not entirely, responsible for what has happened, then you might wisely move into a form of healing other than self-forgiveness. Grieving, directing anger properly, reconsidering your own power, and defining personal boundaries and contracts may improve your life immensely. If you have nothing to forgive yourself for, but other people are insisting that you do, remember: forgiveness is personal. It is intimate and no one's business but your own. It cannot be commanded or demanded. Self-forgiveness is a person's own struggle with the very essence of herself as a human. No one can expect it. Self-forgiveness is a lonely, personal struggle; no one else can engage you in that struggle. That you must do yourself.

Step 2: *Identify the sources of the mistakes you've made*

No one wants to confront fundamental personal flaws, but because injuries arise from personal limitations, meanness, or doing something morally wrong, confrontation with oneself means that a person confronts one, or more, of these mistakes.

During this first phase of self-forgiveness, you will want to look differently at how you have perceived your personal limitations or moral duties. You may find, as Candace did, that her understanding of herself was quite narrow when it came to how she affected other people.

KNOWING YOUR LIMITATIONS

Many people believe they know their limitations, especially those that might hurt others. If people think of limitations, however, only as falling short of some ideal, they might not fully understand the kinds of limitations that result in ruined relationships.

Most people think of various virtues when they consider people as having "good" character. Honesty, generosity, loyalty, and kindheartedness are considered by average people and many philosophers to be "right" in and of themselves. It is a virtue when one tells the truth, or is generous, loyal, and kind. Failure results when a person falls short of these virtues. Limitations, most people believe, reflect these failures. One common limitation is obvious where someone lacks the moral fortitude to always tell the truth, especially when truthtelling will probably result in punishment or losing a personal or professional advantage. Most of us can immediately recognize a friend or acquaintance who, in general, tells the truth, but in difficult situations, falters. Falling short of ideal generosity, loyalty, and veracity is not uncommon.

Connie never told her son that he was adopted. When he found out in high school, he confronted her about her deception. Connie knew that she sometimes lied to protect herself; but she never dreamed that this flaw would cost her her happy family life. Her son simply withdrew into silence; their relationship was never the same. Connie will have to try to forgive her habit, which grew over time, of lying instead of dealing directly with anticipated discomfort of telling the truth.

Excessive Virtues

Limitations of another kind are harder to see and understand. These are limitations that become so *only* after a behavior becomes excessive. These "excessive virtues" are identified in the table below.

TWO TYPES OF LIMITATIONS IN VIRTUE

	LIMITATION A *VIRTUOUS BEHAVIOR*	LIMITATION B *EXCESS*
Loyalty	_____	_____
Truthfulness	_____	_____
Generosity	_____	_____
Kindness	_____	_____

In this table, Limitation A on the left side represents the failure people experience when they fall short of virtuous conduct—that is, when they are not adequately loyal or truthful or generous or kind. Limitation B on the right side represents the condition produced when people exceed the particular virtue and ruin relationships as a result. These kinds of limitations are more difficult to come to grips with and to accept as personal flaws because most people learn that honesty or loyalty, for example, are good at all times. We are not taught that honorable behavior can cause people great pain.

Chuck, a fireman, was well liked and respected. He worked long hours. In addition, he had a wife and three children at home and aging parents for whom he felt responsible. He was also a loyal member of two men's clubs and his baseball team. Myrna, Chuck's wife, often complained that Chuck couldn't "set priorities." He was too "stretched," she said. Chuck, to the contrary, thought that Myrna should respect him as a loyal son, husband (after all, he had no other women), father (he paid for everything), and friend.

One day, Myrna simply said she wanted a divorce. She was unhappy; and it was clear that Chuck could not prioritize his various loyalties. She followed through with considerable speed, never wavering in her determination. She remarried a year later, and, he heard, was very happy.

It has been difficult for Chuck to see that his willingness to be more loyal to some people than others was the essential flaw in his ideas about virtue. Now he cannot forgive himself for his limitation in thinking that he could show equal loyalty to everyone without considering the effect this would have on those who were supposedly the closest to him.

Failure expressed as an excess of virtue can bring down marriages, business relationships, parent-child relationships, and friendships as much as falling short of virtue. You may insist on telling the "absolute truth" (as you experience it) to others, even if the truth works like a dagger on the other. Your generosity may have made a friend feel beholden to you, and in spite of the friend's (or child's) protests, you continue. Limitations, in other words, may take the form of falling short of virtue or of imposing one's "virtues" on others.

Sarah thought her children would always stand by her if she showered them with expensive things. She was profoundly hurt and unable to forgive herself, therefore, when her adult daughter moved out of the state and refused to communicate for several years just to escape her mother's "generosity." What Sarah believed was generous, her children thought controlling. Sarah did not face her own limitations by refusing to listen to other people's perspectives. As she begins to forgive herself for the damage done to her relationships, she will have to face her "overzealous virtuousness" and accept the conclusion that her virtues were destructive to others. Sarah will need to see her flaw clearly to overcome and forgive it.

When you begin the hard task of confronting your limitations, you will have to ask yourself this:

Have I continued to do what I decided was best for myself or another person in spite of protest?

Have I known that one of my flaws might one day harm someone, but simply refused to try to improve or change it?

Have other people told me about my limits, but I did not listen?

Jonas in Chapter 2, who led his family into the mountains, would probably have answered "yes" to at least two of these questions. If a person is honest enough to admit that the damaging characteristics of her own limitations have done permanent harm, she has begun to know what she must now forgive. She has taken the first step of the process.

ADMITTING WHEN WE ARE WRONG

One of the more difficult positions people find themselves in is when they are wrong. Wrongness is a violation of private, public, or religious moral codes; and when people violate these, permanent damage is often the outcome. To forgive yourself for being wrong, you have to accept that you were wrong.

✺

John knew that his religion forbade sexual molestation. He knew his duty to his daughters was to protect them and provide for them. He knew he had vowed to be true to his wife. Still, when his oldest daughter was very young, he began to touch her sexually.

When he began, he knew he was wrong. He felt dirty, but he continued the molestation. Over several years, he convinced himself that what he was doing was right. John told himself that his daughter was not being harmed, and that he and she were emotionally closer because of it. His rationalization developed insidiously and steadily until he was cloaked in grandiose self-delusion. He finally became convinced that he was doing the girl a favor in introducing her to heterosexual experience.

His daughter, who felt more and more guilty, reported his behavior to their mother. She believed her daughter.

John lost everything. He lost his marriage, children, and job. He was referred for treatment and tried hard to understand his behavior. He recognized that he was immature and thought very poorly of himself. Still, he has trouble saying that he was wrong—that he violated a profound moral code among parents and children and people in general; it is morally contemptible to use another person solely for one's own gratification. No person may be used solely as a means to anyone else's end.

✺

John is attempting to forgive himself for what he is convinced is his immaturity. He believes immaturity cost him his family; but if he is really to tackle self-forgiveness in an honest way, he will have to conclude that he was morally wrong, not immature. He transgressed a sacred rule between parents and children—that children are safe from their parents' harm.

Transgressions, we said in Chapter 3, come about as a result of violating personally intricate moral codes or larger codes of conduct to which people believe they should adhere. Some people who have trouble forgiving themselves for doing something "wrong" may feel very guilty but not know exactly what part of a code they violated. Others have no trouble at all acknowledging their moral breaches. A child may believe that it is wrong to talk about family problems with a stranger, so when he tells a school psychologist about his mother's drinking and abuse and the mother finds out, subsequently finding a way to have the psychologist fired, the boy may struggle for years to decide whether his revelation was really wrong.

To do right or be wrong is not cut-and-dried. A soldier may hate himself for doing the right thing by following an officer's orders and slaughtering women and children. He will say, "I know it was wrong, but I did it anyway for a larger good."

In this first phase of self-forgiveness, the actual wrong should be identified along with the moral codes that the wrong breached. In other words, if you believe the lie that broke your relationship with a friend was unforgivable, what moral code or codes did the lie violate? If you acted in repulsive ways during a crisis, what code was abrogated? Part of self-forgiveness lies in rethinking the moral code you have broken and recommitting to the one you will now follow.

When you begin to identify what you did wrong, ask yourself these questions:

Did I knowingly violate an explicit or implicit agreement about what was right and wrong, but hoped not to get caught?
Did I violate a religious code I once believed in?

Did I do something I knew was wrong, but convince myself that there was a good reason for it and that if I were caught, I could use the reason as an excuse or justification?

Tim, who borrowed Nolan's car (Chapter 3) and failed to return it, would have answered "yes" to two of the three questions. He believed that lying and stealing were wrong according to his religion, and he hoped his justification (and excuse) would mollify Nolan. Neither did. Tim was wrong. He lost his oldest and dearest friend.

Candace, who stole money from Ted, knows she was wrong and is beginning to admit it to herself. She, too, would answer "yes" to these questions.

If you answer "yes" to these questions, as Tim and Candace would, you have begun to tear down your defenses and face yourself and your flawed morality. Painful as it may be, honesty is the chief ingredient of self-forgiveness, and now you have begun to revisit it in hopes of healing yourself.

MEANNESS AS MISGUIDED POWER

If being mean has taken such a toll in your life that you have lost precious relationships or hurt others because of it, you probably can no longer deny your capacity for nastiness or cruelty. If you have identified that you have a mean streak, you will want to search for its underlying source. Is it jealousy? Does it result from a sense of deprivation of money or station? Is it normal in your environment? Whatever its source, your meanness has finally worked against you to the point that you have lost something dearer than what you hoped to obtain.

Charlie often got drunk, and when he did, he was told that he said vicious things to people or got into fights. Often he didn't remember these incidents. Once, when Charlie was seventeen, he shot a cat in front of his friends when he was drinking.

Charlie remembers this. Charlie also remembers shooting his son's dog in front of him one night and feeling almost as though his eyes would burst from his head as he heard a vicious diatribe exit his lips toward the boy.

Five years later, Charlie still goes to A.A. meetings. He has done the fifth step (he has admitted to God, himself, and another person the exact nature of his wrongs), and he is willing to make amends to all the people he has harmed. Even so, Charlie has been unable to forgive himself. Charlie knows deep inside that he has been and can still be not only wrong but also deeply mean. He knows his alcoholism did not cause him to hurt others. He is quite capable of that without alcohol.

Charlie, if he is to forgive himself, must look deeper into his character to acknowledge his capacity for meanness and search for its sources. Then he can attempt true self-forgiveness—not for the wrongs committed while drinking, but for the part of his character that resulted in those wrongdoings: his meanness.

If you have been a mean person, ask yourself this:

What has meanness accomplished for me? What have I gotten as a result of it?

To whom have I been mean? When did it start? Why didn't I stop it?

If your meanness is lifelong, but no one rejected you until now, you must now honestly face your cavalier notions of power. If meanness was an occasional characteristic, but this time ended in disaster, you will confront the fact that you crossed a line that has permanently changed your life. You cannot go back, but your honesty may free you to move forward.

Step 2 demands that you confront yourself in the most intimate ways. You will look at yourself and admit, and then begin to accept, that you have allowed something about yourself to permanently damage your relationships with others and send your life off on a course you had not anticipated.

Whatever the source—a limitation, a mistake, a wrongdoing, or meanness—the honesty you have laid down as the foundation of self-forgiveness will provide a firm base for the remainder of the process; for honesty and humility are also self-forgiveness's bricks and mortar.

Step 3: Understand the fundamental assumptions about yourself that have shattered and will need repair

In Chapter 1, six core assumptions that make up people's "assumptive sets" were described. Together, these assumptions allow people to move about comfortably during the course of their lives. The fundamental assumptions in most people's bedrock conceptual system are these:

1. The world is benevolent.
2. The world is meaningful.
3. One's self is worthy.[21]
4. The world is somewhat predictable.
5. We have some control over our lives.
6. There is a principle of justice in the world.

We need to believe these things so fundamentally (to keep our worlds from falling apart) that, when we see something that does not fit, we often ignore it, deny it, or "forget" it. For example, if a woman sees her husband with another woman, but truly believes her marriage is inviolable, she will construe the woman as anything other than a lover so that her assumptive set is not thrown into turmoil.

Traumatic experiences shatter these assumptive sets in such a way that the traumatized person cannot marshal her defenses in time to keep her assumptions from falling apart. When our homes are burglarized or our children become terminally ill or our dearest friends destroy our confidences, people begin to question their old assumptions about the world, God, themselves, and others. The same happens when what we do destroys our important relationships and our worlds.

When a person lies, cheats, physically harms, or betrays others, these behaviors may not, at least initially, destroy the perpetrator's assumptions. One of these assumptions might be "I am a good person even though I may cheat sometimes." Another might be "I live in a good world where my friends and loved ones accept my flaws." Another might be "I live in a world where other people may ruin their lives, but that's because there is something wrong with them. Nothing like that could happen to me." When the person goes so far as to cause an unforgiven injury, though, all these assumptions are suddenly invalidated.

An unforgiven wrongdoer is faced with a new set of assumptions. Additionally, she is responsible for destroying the very beliefs that held her world together. The newly rejected wrongdoer has to face the idea that she may not be a good person after all. She finds that others do not unconditionally love her despite her flaws. She cannot force them or convince them to love her again.

The injurer suddenly understands that other people have not rendered her perceptions of the world as less benevolent—she has. She has ruined her own world. This, she believed before, was the fate of bad or unworthy people. When people are dealt unforgivable blows by other people, their assumptive worlds crumble, and they are required to rethink who they are and what the nature of the world really is. When people deal blows to others, the same sort of trauma begins and prompts the same sort of questions:

Am I a worthy person; if I once was, can I ever be again?
I should have known that if I did (or did not do) that, this terrible thing would happen. I did nothing to prevent it. Can I ever trust my judgment again?
How much control do I really have over other people?
If this is a world where bad people are punished and the good are rewarded, then I must be bad, or the world does not work the way I thought it did.

If God has been with me, how could this happen?

If the world is a good place, I should be able to experience it. All I experience is pain.

When people are hurt by others, they question their own worthiness, the world's orderliness, and the amount of control they have over other people. People who betray others may be shocked to find other people's limits in accepting their flaws. Not only the victims' assumptive worlds explode; the people who wound others also cannot bring their worlds back into order as a result. Injurers who care about the harm they have done have permanently damaged their own belief systems. To heal, they, like victims, will have to build new ones.

Self-forgiveness, like forgiving others, involves rebuilding an assumptive set. At the end of the self-forgiveness process, you will have developed new beliefs about yourself, the world, other people, and the meaning of the world in general. Currently you might think something like this:

1. What I believed about myself I can no longer believe.
2. What I believed about others I can no longer believe.
3. What I believed about the world I can no longer believe.

Over time, you will rebuild these beliefs as you forgive yourself.

Step 4: Understand your feelings about the unforgiven incident

In Part I, numerous feelings were identified as the ways people feel "bad" when they cannot forgive themselves. Regret, guilt, shame, and their various combinations were described. You will be working very hard to reduce, if not extinguish, some of these feelings—regret excluded. However, changes in your thinking will, in all probability, precede changes in your feelings about yourself.

The following table dissects the three major feelings that people who must forgive themselves experience in relationship to the type of event that caused the injury.

FEELING	MUST INVOLVE A MORAL WRONGDOING	MUST INVOLVE PERSONAL ACTION (OR FAILURE TO ACT)	CAN INVOLVE EVENTS NOT ASSOCIATED WITH PERSONAL AGENCY
Guilt	Yes	Yes	No
Regret	Not necessarily	No	Yes
Shame	No	No	Yes

If you are feeling bad, but cannot determine whether you feel shame or guilt, you can see from the table that guilt requires that you did something (that is, personal agency was involved). In comparison, you can feel shame for being some kind of person. A poor child feels shame when she did nothing to cause her poverty. If you took morally wrong action, like Candace, you feel guilt. The actual feelings that you experience are important in self-forgiveness because at some time in the future you will express those feelings to another person or attempt to make amends.

When you are examining your feelings, you will want to recall, as described in Chapter 3, that sometimes when people experience what seems to be guilt or shame it is because guilt and shame are familiar. You may blame yourself for something when there is nothing to blame yourself for because, and only because, the feelings you have are uncomfortable but familiar. Because of this, you may want someone to forgive you or to forgive yourself when you have done nothing wrong.

Ask yourself this: "Are the feelings I have the same feelings I have known all my life? Could I want relief from them so badly that I hold myself accountable and want forgiveness when there is nothing to forgive?"

The feelings you experience, like the source of your mistakes, influence your particular course of self-forgiveness. So, you will need to be as exact as possible about the nature of your experience—feelings included.

Step 5: Understand the barriers you might face when you confront your flaws or failures

The nature of some atrocities that people inflict on one another is so horrendous that, put to a vote, almost any group of civilized people would place certain "crimes" in a separate category by themselves. Hideous or unspeakable atrocities, many philosophers, theologians, and ordinary people believe, should be considered "unforgivable" in the human-to-human sense. No human being should attempt to forgive Hitler or Himmler or Pol Pot, for example. To attempt to forgive these people would reduce the magnitude of their abominations to ordinariness. Where people cannot or should not forgive, God alone is left to that task.

For other "crimes," though, some disagree as to whether ordinary people could or should attempt forgiveness. When Pope John Paul II forgave his would-be assassin, Agca, there was disbelief in some circles. The hordes of people who lined up outside prisons awaiting the deaths of John Wayne Gacy or Gary Gilmore did not believe these people forgivable. Our society, our religions, and our religious leaders send a variety of confusing and mixed messages regarding forgiveness. Many people confuse the official act of pardoning with the intimate and extraordinarily personal act of forgiving. Still, each of us probably has some idea about what we would not, could not, and should not forgive.

If you have engaged in some behavior that is either so heinous as to fall in the "other" category (for example, murder), you face obvious forces that advocate against self-forgiveness. You are surrounded by messages that you should neither be forgiven nor forgive yourself. If, as is more likely, you have done something less destructive than murder, you still may face strong and vocal objections to the idea of self-forgiveness. Various forces in our society struggle to advance their definitions of "unforgivable" behavior.

Among the various supposed "unforgivable" acts are obtaining an abortion; forcing someone to have an abortion; hurting someone while driving drunk; killing a whale, dolphin, sea lion, eagle, etc.; molesting children; assaulting and battering a powerless person; and sexually assaulting a child.*

If resistance to your desire to forgive yourself comes from an uninvolved party—that is, someone other than the person you wounded—you need to recognize that biases against forgiveness may be at work, and you must decide if they are enough to prevent you from proceeding.

Barriers to self-forgiveness are surprisingly prevalent in our largely Judeo-Christian culture. If forgiveness is at the heart of Christianity, its advocates are mystifyingly silent. People who try to forgive themselves must try to hang on to the hope that forgiveness is a way to end hatred; and hatred in any form, even directed toward the self, can do no good.

A second barrier to self-forgiveness is when people have developed an enduring characteristic of blaming themselves for most of their failures. People who do this may have low self-esteem, or be depressed.[22] Others may have an inflated sense of their influence over the affairs of their family members or friends. If self-blame is your personal style of coping with difficulty, you might want to sort through this matter with a professional before you proceed with the process of self-forgiveness.

Possibly you have come to believe that God has turned against you or could not forgive you. More will be said about this in a later chapter. If you are to succeed in forgiving yourself when you believe that God judges you harshly, you will want to revisit your thoughts about your spiritual life. God should not be used as a source of maintaining hatred in any form. If you believe that God would not want you to forgive yourself, you might want to reexamine your relationship to God so that He is not mistakenly used to eternally condemn yourself to self-loathing.

If self-hatred has had the additional effect of reducing your responsibilities to other people (for example, if you cannot forgive yourself for

---

*Various interviewees for this book described professional helpers, parents, religious leaders, their own clergy, and friends warning them very stridently that what they had done was unforgivable. People were asked to leave their church congregations, terminate their therapies, or were belittled and condemned for their beliefs about forgiveness.

your divorce so you avoid your children), you might intuitively understand that self-forgiveness increases responsibility. If this is a barrier, it will have to be confronted. Self-forgiveness frees people from self-hatred, but it does not free them of their responsibilities. In fact, as people forgive themselves, their responsibilities to others might increase.

Finally, not forgiving yourself may have become a habit. Illness, sadness, and a feeling of separateness may have "taken hold" of you as a result of your tendency toward non-forgiveness. It is important that you recognize these symptoms as possible legacies of your unresolved resentments and self-blame.

Once you have recognized the barriers you face as you begin the process of forgiving yourself, you can marshal your efforts to eliminate some of these. Some you may challenge directly. Some you have to talk about with friends or professionals. Unless you identify the barriers to forgiveness and begin to tear them down, it will be very hard for you to proceed.

Summary

The five steps to confronting yourself are independently important in answering the question: What is it about myself that I have to forgive? Naming false mistakes and limitations helps you to go through a process of elimination to determine if you really have anything to forgive yourself for. Understanding your mistakes lets you know whether you are faced with personal limitations that may again cause harm, meanness that will surely harm you and others again, or a wrongdoing that has been difficult to accept. Understanding your shattered assumptions tells you how your beliefs about yourself, others, and your world have been changed, and subsequently which ones must be reconstructed. Identifying your feelings enhances your awareness of feelings you would like to get rid of during the process of self-forgiveness. Finally, understanding the barriers reveals any latent and, possibly, fundamental beliefs regarding what you think should remain unforgiven in yourself or anyone else. It also invites you to identify any people who might attempt to convince you that self-forgiveness is wrong.

Candace looked closely at herself. For the first time, she saw a person capable of moral wrongdoing—both legal and personal. She saw herself as capable of violating a trust between herself and a person she cared for and respected. Candace's assumptions about herself as being "above the fray" and able to play on others' punishments so that she could exonerate herself became excruciatingly clear. For the first time, she felt guilt and remorse and had no one else to blame for experiencing these painful emotions.

Candace knows what she must forgive herself for; and, as happens in any process of great personal change, Candace can begin to change because she is aware that if life is to be more than merely survived, change must take place.

Exercises for Confronting Yourself

The exercises in this section have been developed to help you identify the mistakes you are trying to forgive. Some people choose to do the exercises alone, others with therapists or support groups.

It is difficult to confront your flaws. You may be uncomfortable revealing them to other people. Select the exercises most interesting to you and begin to systematically use them.

Many people enjoy keeping a journal that chronicles their experiences of forgiving. You may want to do the same. In this journal, you can record your responses to the exercises so that you can gauge your progress and note the changes you are undergoing.

Five sets of exercises follow. Each set is designed to help you complete the steps in Phase 1 of self-forgiveness. You may want to complete the exercises in the order in which they come, or select one at a time from each section to complete. You may also want to vary them somewhat if you are working with a therapist or in a support group.

These exercises are designed to help you confront the sources of your unforgiven predicament. Exercises 1 through 4 are designed to help you name any false limitations or wrongdoings that may lead you to believe you have to forgive yourself, when you really have nothing to forgive.

Exercise 1: Did I Do Something Wrong?
Think about the first time you realized you had unforgivably hurt the person whom you believe you injured. Then ask yourself these questions:

1. Did I know, before anyone else told me, that I had wounded someone because of my flaws or transgressions?
2. Was I aware that one of my flaws might one day harm someone? How?

Sometimes your mistakes can give other people power over you. In this next exercise, think about the ways your hurting the someone who will not forgive you gave him or her power over you.

Exercise 2: Injury as Power
Complete these incomplete thoughts:

A. Because I think I hurt _____, he or she now has the power to:
    1.
    2.
    3.

B. Since I have come to think that I hurt _____, I now volunteer to do a number of things for her (him) that I did not used to do. Some of these are:
    1.
    2.
    3.

Other people often do not see you as having done something wrong. In the next exercise, try to think of everyone who has told you that you should not blame yourself.

Exercise 3: Are People Trying to Tell Me Something?
1. List anyone who has told you that your mistakes, wrongdoings, or limitations were not the cause of someone else's harm.
2. List the reasons you reject their ideas.
3. Are there aspects of the situation of which these people are not aware?

You may be a person who tends to blame herself for many things you do. If so, complete this next exercise.

Exercise 4: The Blame Habit
A. Think of the person your wrongdoing harmed. List as many incidents as you can remember where this person blamed you before. She/he blamed me for
   1.
   2.
   3.
   4.
   5.

B. Think of a time when you blamed her/him. Write them down.

C. Is there a pattern where this person has blamed you over time, more than you have blamed him or her?

Exercises 5 through 8 are designed to help you understand limitations that you will need to change. Limitations may be physical, emotional, or intellectual. If you have a "blind spot" to any one of these, use the following exercises to help see them more clearly.

Exercise 5: Sensory Limitations

Listed here are the five senses. Any of these can change in their acuity as people age or become temporarily ill. Do you have any social limitations because of sensory troubles? (For example, do you have trouble in conversations because you do not hear well?)

	DOES ANY LIMITATION EXIST?	ARE THERE ANY SOCIAL LIMITATIONS?
Sight		
Hearing		
Sense of Smell		
Touch		
Taste		

Where you experience social limitations because of sensory troubles, are the limitations bad enough to harm your relationships?

Exercise 6: Physical Limitations

Many people believe they are stronger than they really are. Do you have any evidence that you overestimate your strength? Has this overestimation ever hurt anyone? Describe one example of this.

Exercise 7: Moral Limitations—The Breaking Point

A. Most people who concern themselves with forgiveness are interested in, and aware of, morality. On the following list of moral virtues, think about the point at which you might not absolutely adhere to "moral" behavior. Describe the circumstance where you might not follow through on each.

	EXCEPTION
1. Truth-telling	
2. Loyalty	
3. Generosity	
4. Kindness	

Has falling short of truthfulness, loyalty, kindness, or generosity ever resulted in interpersonal problems?

B. Has being too honest, generous, kind, or loyal ever gotten you into trouble? Describe the situations in detail. Do you see any patterns?

Exercise 8: Limitations in Accurately Rating Your Talents or Knowledge

People often can function more than adequately where their talents or intellectual abilities are concerned. It takes only one experience of over-rating one of these to know the pain that overrating can cause. (In Chapter 2, for example, Jonas thought he knew more about mountain conditions than he really did. His overrating his knowledge nearly cost him and his family their lives.)

1. List any talent or area of knowledge that you were told you were overconfident about.
2. Has your overrating ever hurt a relationship?
3. Have you secretly tried to cover up your limitations? How?

Limitations may not be a person's fault. That is, a person probably does not intend—or even expect—a limitation to result in injuries to others. Because limitations are common to unforgiven injuries, they should be faced squarely. If you have other flaws that may result in harm to others, take time to identify them now.

The next series of exercises is designed to help you think about any moral code you may have broken. Sometimes people believe that they have done something wrong when, in fact, they have not. These exercises should help you see whether your inability to forgive yourself really stems from some wrong you have done or from other mistakes you have made.

Exercise 9: The Moral Law

A. A moral law underlies all your important relationships. It sets the limits regarding what you consider acceptable and unacceptable treatment of each other. In the relationship you believe you harmed, try to identify the moral law between you and the injured person. Start with promise-keeping. Identify the exceptions you believe you both tacitly or explicitly agreed to.

EXCEPTIONS TO PROMISE-KEEPING

I believed I could break a promise to you under the following conditions:

You believed you could break a promise to me under the following conditions:

EXCEPTIONS TO TRUTH-TELLING

I agreed that you could lie to me under the following conditions:

You agreed I could lie to you under the following conditions:

EXCEPTIONS TO FULL DISCLOSURE

I agreed to fully disclose any mutually important information except under the following conditions:

You agreed to fully disclose important information except under the following conditions:

B. After you examine the terms of the moral agreement you had developed with the person you hurt, do you believe you transgressed the terms of your contract? That is, do you believe you did something wrong?

Exercise 10: The Larger Moral Code

Most people live by a moral code larger than the ones they have developed with the people in their lives. It is likely that the specific moral laws between people reflect very personal interpretations of larger codes such as the Ten Commandments or other religious proscriptions. In this exercise, identify any larger moral imperatives that you believe you should follow. (An example might be that it is a duty to honor your father and mother.)

1. List these imperatives.
2. After each imperative is identified, list circumstances when it might be acceptable to violate the imperative. (An example for some people might be that it is acceptable not to honor parents if they abuse their children.)
3. When you hurt the people or person who will not or cannot forgive you, did you violate a moral imperative in an unacceptable way?

Meanness is the third source of perpetrating an unforgiven act. The next exercises are suggested to let you identify if meanness has resulted in your current inability to forgive yourself.

Exercise 11: Normative Meanness

Some children are socialized in groups where cruelty and nastiness are valued.

1. Write a paragraph on what you thought about mean people in grade school, and then in high school.
2. Do you currently have friends who are particularly mean? What do you like about these people?

Exercise 12: Jealous Meanness

Think of any time when you were jealous.

1. What did you do to the person you were jealous of?
2. What were the results?
3. Did your action give you satisfaction?

Exercise 13: The Quick Tongue

Do you have a quick tongue that you use to control or hurt people?

1. How did you come to have this?
2. Has it done you more harm than good?
3. What is the worst result of your "quick tongue" so far?

People you have harmed have been damaged by your limitations, wrongness, or nastiness. It is important, then, for you to understand which of the three it was. To change any of the three requires developing strategies to change them and the sheer determination to work at it.

Regrettably, when a person betrays himself to the point he cannot forgive himself, he shatters key assumptions that have held his world together. These assumptions are about himself, other people, and the world. The next exercises will help you identify your shattered assumptions so that you can begin to reconstruct them.

Exercise 14: Before and After Assumptions

Complete these thoughts:

1. a. Before I behaved in the way I did, I believed these things about myself:
   b. Since that time, I have come to believe (complete the sentence)
   _____.

2. a. Before this experience, I believed these things about other people, (specifically the person you harmed):
   b. Since that time, I have come to believe _____.

3. a. Before this experience, I believed these things about my religion and God:
   b. Since that time, I have come to believe _____.

Exercise 15: Why I Should Forgive Myself

In this exercise, write down all the reasons you have identified so far that convince you that you should forgive yourself. List sources of your mistakes, broken moral codes, and your current beliefs about yourself. This will be an important "anchor exercise" for the rest of your forgiveness work.

Finally, this last exercise is designed to assist you in identifying the feelings you harbor. Among them may be guilt, grief, shame, remorse, anger, and regret. You will, over time, change some or all of these feelings.

Exercise 16: The Adjective Collage

Look through magazines and newspapers for words that describe how you feel about yourself. When you see an adjective that describes you, cut it out of the magazine and place it in an envelope you keep for the purpose.

On a piece of cardboard, glue the cut-out words. Be creative! If you want, use magic markers or colored pens to make your collage more artistic.

Keep the collage where only you can see it. Later in the self-forgiveness process, you may want to share it with a counselor or friend.

Exercises for Understanding Barriers to Forgiving Yourself

You have come to the point of needing to forgive yourself with certain beliefs about forgiveness in general. The following exercises are designed to help you recognize if any of these beliefs (or people) will impede your progress toward forgiving yourself.

Exercise 17: Crimes Beyond Forgiveness

Think of the circumstance for which you need to forgive yourself. Now ask yourself this set of questions:

1. If a good friend of yours did this to an acquaintance of hers, would you tell her to forgive herself? Why or why not?
2. If your friend did this to you, would you want her to forgive herself? Would you believe what she did was forgivable even if you could not forgive her?
3. If put to a vote of a hundred randomly chosen people, do you think a majority would vote that what you did was forgivable?
4. If your "case" was tried in a court of law, could the defense offer up an argument that might lead to a "not guilty" verdict?
5. Is there any case in literature like yours? How did you feel about the character who behaved the way you did?

Exercise 18: Self-Blame as Part of Your Character

A barrier to forgiving yourself might be that you are very hard on yourself and forgive yourself for very little. Holding yourself in exile and blaming yourself may have become part of your character. Self-blame can also be associated with the false belief that you control more aspects of life, in general, than you really do. Try this exercise:

Think of the major losses you have experienced in your life. List them and rate from 1 to 5 how much you blame yourself for each loss. 1 means almost you are not at all to blame; 3 means you are somewhat to blame; and 5 means you are completely to blame. How badly did you blame yourself? Do you see any patterns? Are there some kinds of past losses for which you are less likely to blame yourself than others?

	Loss	*Score*
1.		
2.		
3.		

Exercise 19: The Importance of Self-Blame

Has anyone ever told you that you were not to blame and you felt annoyed or upset? What were the circumstances? Why was blaming yourself so important? How did you work out your feelings with the other person?

Exercise 20: Hidden Non-Forgiveness
Your parents, friends, spouse, or others close to you may not believe in forgiving in any form or only under certain circumstances. In this exercise, write the names of the people who could influence your process of self-forgiveness. In a column next to each name, try to write down what you think each person believes about forgiveness. Finally, try to think of a situation in which one person demonstrated forgiveness toward another.

Now, with a "yes" or "no," write down whether you believe each of these people would encourage you to forgive yourself.

Exercise 21: Responsibility Check
In all probability, the losses you experienced when you damaged your relationship(s) included losses of responsibility. You may not have had to help out the person you hurt, even if she asked. Were you overly responsible to the person you hurt? Because you have felt so bad about yourself, are there any responsibilities you have dropped? What are they?

Summary

The first phase of forgiving yourself involves taking the steps to understand exactly what it is you are attempting to forgive. Some people may find, after taking these steps, that they feel guilty, but they can find no moral law they violated. Some may feel ashamed, but can find no limitation that is the basis for their sense of shame. Many people feel badly about themselves for no specific reason. Others carry guilt as a constant companion.

If this is the case for you, it is good to find out that you have nothing to be forgiven for. You may want to talk with someone about your bad feelings, but not direct your energy toward self-forgiveness.

If you have concluded that you indeed did violate a moral pact or allowed your limitations to harm people or were mean enough to ruin a relationship, once you have completed the first phase of self-forgiveness, you know what you are up against. You know the mistakes you have made, the assumptions you must reconstruct, and the barriers you must face. You see the internal enemies and understand the external impediments.

Now you can move forward.

CHAPTER 6

Holding Yourself Responsible

Rachel left Oakacres that November night angry, exhausted, and overwhelmed. Twice during the day, her mother had had to be put in restraints. She had torn out her IVs and tried to pull the respirator tube out. To Rachel, the end of a four-year nightmare seemed to finally be approaching, but the nurses had assured her that the best thing she could do was to go home and rest.

Alzheimer's disease had taken a toll on the entire Rosen family. Rachel's brother played his usual game— "I don't know how to help"—and except when the fifty-two-year-old Rachel gave her fifty-year-old "little brother" direct instructions, he didn't. Rachel's husband, Ben, had tried to support her, and usually did; but he was not able to muster the courage to demand that their children, now nearly grown, not exact so much of Rachel's waning emotional reserves. They had become entirely self-involved. They would not, or could not, see that their grandmother was slipping away, and that Rachel often felt so fully depleted she wondered if she would die first.

Rachel had made a solemn vow to herself, though. She vowed she would see her mother through her terrible illness and never, under any circumstances, let her die alone.

That November night, one of her children, Ruth, had come over to find comfort from Rachel and to weep again about her boyfriend. Ruth was inconsolable. Rachel listened to Ruth for more than an hour. She called the hospital about midnight to learn that her mother was having more severe breathing difficulties. Rachel started for her purse to leave for the hospital, but Ruth increased her whimpering. Rachel called her brother to ask him to go to the hospital, but he refused; he had an important meeting the next morning.

At 12:45, the attending nurse to Rachel's mother called to tell her that her mother was suffering from labored breathing and tachycardia. Rachel raced to the hospital, but as she entered her mother's room she heard the sound of the heart monitor stabilize into a single tone.

Rachel felt a part of herself die at that moment; and the part that lives, she has never forgiven.

Rachel is bitterly confused about her mother's death. She is guilty; and she is angry at her brother and her husband. She resents her adult children for not trying to be adults at a time when she needed their maturity and support more than ever before. Rachel feels that she will have to forgive herself to be able to go on with her life, but she also believes that she should not have been put in such a position in the first place. Her brother, who seems at peace with the way he handled the situation, feels none of her guilt; nor does he understand hers.

Rachel's anger, resentment, and guilt have impeded her attempts to forgive herself for more than a year. Her confusion dominates her days when she continually wonders how responsible she really was for her mother's dying alone. Rachel knows she broke a sacred promise, but she also believes fervently that

*had her family members acted differently, she could have, and
would have, been at her mother's side.*

⟶≈⟵

Phase 2 of self-forgiveness is holding yourself responsible. The overarching purpose of this phase is to clarify who is responsible, and to what
degree, for the situation a person cannot forgive himself for. Clarity is
essential to forgiveness. Phase 2 engages the person in need of forgiveness in more active exploration of, and confrontation with, the situation
that caused him so much pain. When you explore a situation and your
own part in it, your true emotions about it and yourself are revealed.

Self-forgiveness is a process of revelation and surrender, maintaining
and rebuilding—not a process of conquest over feelings. You will want
to surrender to your feelings, not to conquer them. During Phase 2, it is
best to remember: *You cannot forgive yourself until you are convinced it is
you who needs to be forgiven.*

In some cases, the identification of a person who is responsible for
an injury is a simple matter. For example, if a red-faced furious mother
hits her two-year-old in the face, she probably holds herself totally
responsible for her behavior. If the child were older, though, and bel-
ligerent, assaultive, and defiant, the situation becomes more complex
because most children have been taught how to control angry impulses,
and, unlike infants, are able to intentionally hurt others. The mother who
hits this child can tell herself she was pushed too far, or that her mouthy
child shared some responsibility for the incident. No doubt this woman
could find some support for her position from friends or neighbors. The
second mother might hold herself less responsible than the first mother
because there were factors, she believes, that provoked her to strike
her child.

A third mother hits her child with a baseball bat when he comes at
her with a chair. The third mother feels even less responsible than the
first two. She has a justification for her behavior that may help her forgive herself more easily.

Self-forgiveness is intimately related to the level of responsibility a person accepts for what he has done. Therefore, it is essential that a person accurately assign responsibility for what he has done, even to determine that he was not really responsible, and as a result, does not need to forgive himself. Often, forgiving someone else might be in order.

Holding yourself responsible has three steps:

1. Identify any complications that might make the assignment of responsibility difficult.
2. Learn a way to assign responsibility.
3. Uncover any secrets that may lie at the heart of a person's inability to forgive himself. (Secrets can shield a person from accepting responsibility.)

During the second phase of self-forgiveness, you continue coming face-to-face with yourself so that you can see yourself in an honest light—limitations, meanness, and all. Like forgiving others, self-forgiveness is not for cowards. It is for only the bravest among us.

Step 1: Identify any complications that might make the assignment of responsibility difficult

When assigning responsibility for an unforgiven injury, or any incident for that matter, a number of powerful complicating factors can explain how each person might see an incident in a slightly different light. Two people who witness a traffic accident will, in all likelihood, see different things. Each person processes the experiences he sees, hears, touches, or smells through his own "filter." This "filter" includes his culture, ethnic group, religious heritage, age, gender, family constellation, and area of his country in which he was raised (to name a few complicating factors).

If two people see a married couple exchanging loud words, a woman from Florida might interpret the exchange very differently from a man from Egypt. The same is true when people assign responsibility to other people for the activities they are engaged in. For precisely this reason, many accused people would rather be tried by a jury than a judge. The diversity of people on a jury is sure to result in a variety of conclusions regarding personal responsibility.

A relatively large body of research exists on factors that affect the assigning of responsibility, and readers may want to explore this research in more detail than is necessary here (see Appendix). For self-forgiveness as it is related to assigning responsibility, three complicating factors only will be explored:

1. Models of assigning responsibility in a person's family of origin
2. Religious orientation
3. Gender

MODELS OF ASSIGNING RESPONSIBILITY IN YOUR FAMILY OF ORIGIN

When you think about the household(s) in which you were raised, you probably can identify some of the "lessons" you learned about responsibility. You might have experienced membership in a family like the "Tough family."

The "Tough family" emphasizes that each person takes responsibility for his or her own failures. When a Tough family member fails, all its members agree that the failure was a result of some internal attribute of the person who failed and not a result of outside influences. In the Tough family, everyone thinks that a person who failed should have prepared better or worked harder. Personal successes are also presumed to be due to something internal. When Ann Tough got a promotion because she passed a written test, congratulations were offered and praise showered on Ann by the entire family for her hard work. No one considered that Ann was lucky or that the test was simple.

Unlike the Toughs, the "Wegood family" has adopted a style where failure is assigned to individuals as an internal matter, but individual success is thought to be a result of outside influences. A Wegood family member's success is thought to be externally caused. When Joe Wegood failed the test that Ann Tough passed, the Wegood family assumed that Joe did not study hard enough, or, worse, was not smart enough to make the mark. However, when Joe gave a rousing speech at the Rotary Club, no one in the family said, "You did well because you worked so hard." Instead, Joe's elderly mother said, "Everyone in the Wegood family does well when we have to—we are winners." In the Wegood family, children learn that successes are always attributed to something other than an individual's commitment to a task or level of trying.

A close cousin to the Wegoods is the "Goodluck family." To the Goodlucks, failure is an internal matter, but success is out of a person's hands. A Goodluck family member does well on a test, public performance, or competition because "luck smiled" on the Goodluck member; or the planets might have been aligned in a certain way.

The "Angst family" never understands why things go so badly for them. When Mrs. Angst went for a job interview at a bank in jeans and without makeup, she could not understand why she was turned down. Her horoscope had predicted a good day; so Mrs. Angst wondered if she should consult a different newspaper's psychic. Mr. Angst was recently demoted at work. He thinks his bosses conspired against him and maybe one of his fellow employees set out to take his job. He tells Mrs. Angst he was demoted because she was rude to the boss's wife at the last Christmas party. Both Mr. and Mrs. Angst are confused.

The Angst children, watching their parents, wonder if there is a hex on their house. They have heard their grandmother say so; they wonder too, if, as grandmother recommends, some healer should drive away the hex with sage smoke.

The Angst family attributes the sources of their troubles to external or unstable people and forces. As a result, they are at a loss as to how to prevent misfortune or assure success.

The Angst family's close cousins are the "Merlin family." The Merlins, like the Angsts, know that there is a hex on them. So although the Merlins know that their troubles are beyond their control, they at least believe that the source of trouble is external and stable. When they find the source of the hex, they will be able to fight back and end their troubles.

There are many family approaches to assigning responsibility from which children learn how to think about success and failure, and, more importantly, how to prevent failure and ensure success. A person who learns that personal effort or commitment has little to do with success believes that he has few internal methods for preventing personal failure. Someone who, by contrast, looks to himself for the source to all success and failure may not have learned the limits to his own control over life's happenings.

Finally, some children may learn that one person in their family is responsible for all its troubles. Children may watch an alcoholic blame his spouse, for example, for his personal and professional problems instead of attributing them to his excessive drinking. A spouse may blame her husband for her unhappiness, when she was unhappy long before their marriage. Children who see the externalization of trouble and failure often become masters at it themselves.

The way that people learn to attribute trouble to either internal or external sources can affect self-forgiveness in a profound way: Some people who cannot forgive themselves hold themselves accountable for situations over which they had little control; and some people who cannot forgive themselves have trouble knowing what, exactly, their contribution to the unforgiven event was.

᠁

Melissa Angst and Tom Tough each hit a pedestrian. Tom Tough is inconsolable. Even though the police have told him that the pedestrian had a long history of walking out from between parked cars into traffic, Tom believes he should have been quicker with his brakes or more vigilant. Tom cannot accept that his control over the "accident" was minimal. Melissa feels extremely bad about herself, too. Her horoscope had said Thursday would be an unlucky day. Because she hit the pedestrian on Thursday, she thinks she will have to forgive herself for not following the advice of her psychic reader. (Actually Melissa needs new glasses because her eyesight is dangerously bad, but Melissa has learned that bad things are not personally in her control.)

Learned styles of attribution are intriguing and complex. Many of us can think of family members who have tried to teach us (or have taught us) that bad things are brought on by unknown forces, ghosts, evil spirits, black cats, or curses. How you think about painful happenings is probably a result of watching and listening to the adults around you as they responded to family illnesses, deaths, accidents, divorces, and job problems. Rachel knows that in her family, failure is interpreted as a result of a lack of effort. Because she understands her family's influence, she can synthesize it into her interpretation of her mother's death.

When you are in the unwelcome and painful position of not being able to forgive yourself, you will need clarity regarding what you are and are not responsible for. A careful analysis of your family's style of attributing responsibility in times of trouble will help you discard any pattern you may have learned from them that is making self-forgiveness difficult.

RELIGIOUS TEACHINGS AND ASSIGNING RESPONSIBILITY

Each of us who has been raised in a home or homes where religion is important has probably been influenced by religious interpretations of the sources and causes of fortune and misfortune. Some interpretations of Biblical scripture assign people's misfortune and pain to internal and stable characteristics of human beings. In some religious sects, all people are sinners, and all troubles due to sin. In other sects, some people are wicked; some good. Scriptures like those that follow assign trouble to humans, regardless of whether it is distributed evenly among the righteous and the wicked.

No ills befall the righteous, but the wicked are filled with trouble. (Proverbs 12:21)

Surely God wrongs not men, but themselves men wrong. (Koran 10:44)

God changes not what is in a people, until they change what is in themselves. (Koran 13:11)

Misfortune pursues sinners, but prosperity rewards the righteous. (Proverbs 13:21)

The struggle to frame and explain God's role, intentions, and motives in a world of suffering has been a central theme of theological writing, from the writings of Gautama to the book of Job in the Bible to *When Bad Things Happen to Good People.*[23] How could a loving, merciful God watch good people suffer or children die of starvation? If God does not have a hand in the pain people experience, could it be that He is also not responsible for life's blessings?

Some people who need to forgive themselves have been taught that God punishes people for their sins; God is perceived to be the external and stable source of suffering in some religious traditions. The books of Isaiah and Ezekiel are replete with descriptions of God's displeasure and fury. Some people believe that God watches his children cause each other pain and awaits their confessions so that He can forgive them. Whether God causes suffering or has little to do with it is a question that may plague people who cannot forgive themselves. In the first case, people might conclude that if their suffering is caused by God as punishment for their sins, they should not forgive themselves. To do so would be presumptuous. In the second case, self-forgiveness might seem more in line with God's will; if people can restore peace where there is hatred, God is pleased.

The Vietnam war veteran who killed women and children might blame and hate himself. He might also blame and hate his commanding officer. He could detest politicians whose decisions allowed the war to continue. But the veteran may feel uncomfortable, saying that he also hates God because God did not intervene, or because the good person that he had been was sullied forever in the eyes of God when he took another person's life. The veteran may reason that he was not wicked until the war entered his life and that now he is the recipient of God's punishment.

Religion can be an integral factor in how people assign responsibility to themselves, other people, or external forces for their well-being and their suffering. Rachel realizes that in her religious tradition (at least, as it has been taught to her), that bad things happen to people because God reads the minds of the unworthy and punishes them for their unworthy thoughts. Because she has learned this, Rachel wonders if God took her mother at the moment he did in order to punish her.

If how you think about personal suffering has been deeply affected by your religious views, you will want to sort out these views to assess the impact they are having on your experiences. If you do not believe you can or should forgive yourself without God's first forgiving you, this is the time to recognize your belief. Different people will follow different paths to self-forgiveness.

GENDER AND ASSIGNING RESPONSIBILITY

Women may hold themselves more accountable for their failures and flaws than men.[24] Women engage in the internal attribution of failure because of a combination of family, religious, educational, and historical influences. A wife whose husband has an affair may hate herself because she thinks her aging body became unattractive to him. She may tell herself that she should have gone to the gym or played more tennis. She might hold herself responsible for not learning how to fix more interesting low-fat dishes or undergoing liposuction for her "cottage cheese" thighs. A man in the same circumstance is more likely to blame his wife or the "other man" for the affair than to attribute its cause to himself.

Women assign responsibility for failures to internal and stable personal characteristics more often than men do. They might blame themselves for not being smart enough, thin enough, social or fun enough. When women try to forgive themselves, they may have a more difficult time disconnecting themselves from the situation because of their general style of attributing failure to personal flaws and limitations.

Rachel knows that women in her family hold themselves more responsible for family affairs than men do. Her grandmother, mother, and sisters blame themselves when there is family trouble more than do her grandfather, father, and brothers. Understanding the family tradition of women taking responsibility for interpersonal matters, Rachel will use the knowledge to comprehend her role in her mother's death. She may hold herself responsible for not being with her mother when she died, and she will not be able to separate the event of her mother's death from other situations that she has habitually believed she was responsible for. As Rachel proceeds through self-forgiveness, though, she will revise her sense of responsibility and distribute it more evenly among her brother, husband, and daughter.

Family modeling, religious upbringing, and gender each affect personal patterns of assigning responsibility for different events in a person's life. Some readers may find that they are trying to forgive themselves for circumstances they really had little or nothing to do with. Others may conclude that trying to forgive themselves has been so difficult because they believe they are sinners and deserve to suffer; self-forgiveness would be an affront to God.

Rachel examined the impact of her family and her religious beliefs on the way she assigns responsibility to herself. She concluded that her family believed that all happenings, good and bad, are directly related to how hard a person tries. She recognizes that her religious tradition holds individuals accountable for their own suffering. Rachel perceives that because of these influences, she often feels responsible when she should not. Having determined this, she can proceed to the next step of self-forgiveness and learn whether, when she actually attempts to assign responsibility to someone for her mother's dying alone, she or someone else is most responsible.

Step 2: Learn a new way to assign responsibility

After you have completed Step 1 and identified complicating factors that affect the way you assign responsibility in general, you are ready to address specific questions about the situation that remains unforgiven. Because at this point in the process of self-forgiveness it is clear whether the damage resulted from a limitation or a transgression, you must ask yourself one of two sets of questions. The first set can be asked by a person whose limitations injured other people and themselves. The second set can be asked by a person who transgressed moral or legal boundaries.

QUESTIONS TO ASK WHEN YOU CONSIDER LIMITATIONS AND ASSIGN RESPONSIBILITY

Ask yourself the following questions if you fell short of a virtue, exceeded a virtue, or had some other limitation that resulted in harm:

1. Before the unforgiven events, was I aware that I had this limitation?
2. Did I know that this limitation could result in harm?
3. If I knew that this limitation could result in harm, did I try to correct or improve it?
4. Could the harm that occurred have taken place whether my limitation were present or not?

The answer to question 1 reveals whether an unforgiven person was self-aware. Answers to questions 2 and 3 reveal whether he could have foreseen that his flaws could one day do damage. Question 4's answer tells if the relationship between the limitation and the damage was causal or circumstantial. Answering these questions is important, not because the answers reveal that someone is or is not responsible, but because the answers reveal to what degree a person is responsible.

Responsibility is not a black-and-white, either/or concept. A person is not totally responsible or totally not-responsible. Responsibility can be assigned by degree, the lowest being when a person is barely responsible; the highest being when there is no question that a person played a major part in bringing some circumstance about. Degrees of responsibility can be put on a scale from "least responsible" to "most responsible," and a person can place himself on that scale. A person who intends something to happen and takes action to make it happen is more responsible than a person who could have foreseen that something might happen, but took no steps to stop it. Intentionality is nearly the highest level of responsibility, and foreseeability is the next lower level.

Limitations are, by definition, not intentional, but we all have different levels of awareness about our limitations and whether they can cause harm.

Jonas (Chapter 2) set out to answer the four questions. He knew his arrogance and unwillingness to listen to others contributed to his family's near-tragedy, but he could not convince himself that Julie was not as responsible as he for the mishap. At times, he even convinced himself he should try to forgive her instead of himself. (Most of us do this to avoid the pain of the entire burden of guilt or shame we feel.)

Jonas looked at question 1. He told himself that his stubbornness was a virtue, but a virtue that, in excess, might become a flaw. He had known this prior to his family's trip to the mountains. Next, in answer to question 2, he had to admit that during his marriage, he had hurt his family, particularly Julie, because of his bull-headedness. Once, he recalled, she had become quite ill after swallowing a medication he insisted she take and that she resisted. When she protested, he belittled her judgment relentlessly until she gave in to his demands. Jonas knew he could cause harm because Julie had been sick for days afterward. He could, in other words, foresee that his arrogance and willfulness were capable of hurting people.

Knowing that he could hurt people, Jonas did nothing to temper his penchant for not taking others' judgments into consideration. His answer to question 3 was "no." He sought no professional help, talked to no one about his character flaws, and refrained from any self-scrutiny that might have lowered his opinion of himself.

When answering question 4, Jonas would like to have told himself that he need not have been present for his family to go off into the mountains that day. He tried to convince himself that they might have been with a hiking club instead, or that the boys could have been on a school field trip. But he simply could not deceive himself that, in other conditions, the family would have found themselves together in jeopardy of freezing to death. Unhappily, Jonas concluded that the near-tragedy would not have happened in his absence. His flaws were directly associated with the events that day and not circumstantial to them.

When Jonas proceeds toward self-forgiveness, it will become clearer to him that he will attempt to forgive himself not because he was unaware of his shortcomings and failures. He was not unaware. He will try to forgive himself because he had recognized for some time that he might really hurt someone some day, but did not value this recognition enough to try to improve himself for the sake of his loved ones. Jonas has had a shock to his "value system," but it is not too late for him to place his values in a far different order.

Rachel, like Jonas, was aware that she failed to set limits on people around her. She did not say "no" often enough, to her children particularly. To question 2, she also answered "yes." She had come to believe that her flaw had had a bad impact on her children. Over time, Ruth, particularly, had shown herself to be unable to cope with ordinary disappointments in life and to make decisions regarding them. Rachel, sorrowfully, believes that her flaw resulted in her children's dependency on her. Unlike Jonas, though, Rachel had sought help. She had talked with friends and taken a class in "assertiveness." Rachel knew her continuation of setting no limits on her children could do them more damage. So she tried to change.

Question 4 is the one that troubles Rachel. If she had not allowed Ruth to demand her attention the night of her mother's death, might her mother have died alone in some other circumstances anyway? Rachel decided that there were, indeed, other situations that could have resulted in the same sad experience. Rachel might have been out of town, for example, or with her husband at a long-awaited weekend away that had been planned for months. Rachel's inability to set limits on her children was not the cause of her mother's lonely death. The death could have happened another way. As Rachel moves forward in her self-forgiveness, she can take comfort that she was aware of one of her limitations and that it did not play the most significant role in her unabating guilt and grief. She will find, however, when she takes Step 3 and uncovers her secrets that her pain is not abated because of a secret she can barely admit to herself, let alone share with someone else.

Limitations that are at the source of unforgiven situations may have been unrecognized, recognized but not improved, or circumstantial to the unforgiven situation. This is not the situation when transgressions result in unforgiven injuries.

QUESTIONS TO ASK WHEN YOU CONSIDER TRANSGRESSIONS AND ASSIGNING RESPONSIBILITY

Because transgressions are intentional and engaged in specifically by a person to benefit himself, there is no doubt that the person knows he is transgressing. A person who tries to forgive himself for a transgression cannot delude himself that he was unaware of what he was doing or that, if discovered, the transgression could harm another person or himself.

Questions about transgressions are not about foreseeability. Instead, they are about whether the transgressor has a habit of committing wrongdoings or whether the unforgiven wrongdoing was a one-time occurrence. A habitual transgressor lives a life of painful self-indulgence, hoping not to be discovered. A one-time transgressor engages in an act that is planned to bring about personal gratification; he also hopes not to be exposed. When you examine the wrongdoing that precipitated the unforgiven situation, ask yourself these three questions:

1. Have I broken moral rules more than a few times? Has wrongdoing become a way of life?
2. When I transgressed, what did I value more than the law or rule I betrayed?
3. Did I intend to harm when I transgressed?

Candace, who stole money from her boss, addressed these questions. She answered "no" to questions 1 and 3, and turned her attention to question 2, to which she answered, "Having money to buy things meant more to me than the consequences of my actions." Candace recounted the desires behind her stealing in these words:

> *"I knew what I was doing. That's the hard part. When I left my grandparents' home, I never had enough money, but instead of getting another job or asking for a loan, I just started stealing.*
>
> *"I think now that I valued 'having stuff' more than I valued my reputation or my grandparents' feelings. Maybe, I even tried to hurt them—I don't know—by hurting their reputation. It was hard, after being raised in such a Christian place, to admit that what mattered to me most was stuff."*

Candace is beginning to recognize that she does not have an intact moral life or a clear sense of what she values. She sees that right and wrong change in definition depending on what she desires. If she desires to have "stuff," then stealing becomes right. Candace has lost all self-respect and the respect of her grandparents. Her journey of self-forgiveness will force her to rethink her desires and whether she will continue to transgress to fulfill them.

Kurt (Chapter 4), unlike Candace, did not habitually break the moral codes of an important relationship. His driving drunk, until the accident, took nothing from any specific individual, as lying or stealing does. But Kurt, in habitually violating the law, transgressed against society rather than a particular person.

When Kurt attempts this second phase of self-forgiveness, he will be challenged to forgive a person who was hedonistic and narcissistic at the possible expense of strangers. His own pleasures were more important than any other individual's rights. Kurt answered "yes" to question 1. He regularly broke the law, but he did not value things so much as the "freedom" to feel drunk and to drive drunk. He did not mean to harm (question 3), but his freedom was more important to him than the possibility of harming someone.

Mary Lee (Chapter 3), in contrast to Kurt, decided her affair with the Reverend Smith was more important than the damage it might bring her husband, family, and marriage. The affair elevated her hedonism and narcissism to a place of value over her husband's feelings. She will try to forgive herself for being a person who could diminish another person's worth so easily. Mary Lee's answer to question 2 is repulsive to her because it reveals a selfishness she had never acknowledged.

A person who transgresses once is like Kim, who lied to her sister Karen about where she was going to wear the dress she borrowed. Kim, not an habitual transgressor, sees that her chance to meet a man to whom she was attracted was more important to her than her relationship with her sister. She is jarred to find that she lost sight of her values and must attempt to forgive herself for her moral "slip."

Whether your situation is one that forces you to confront your habit of transgressing or your willingness to breach morality to get what you want, you are now in a position to stop deluding yourself about your values and to confront them openly.

People who intentionally cause harm to acquire what they want answer "yes" to question 3. They are different from other wrongdoers because when they violate moral codes or rules they inflict physical pain on others. Robert's evil transgressions are difficult for outsiders to understand, but a counselor in the boy's facility in which he is incarcerated began to understand and guide him toward self-forgiveness.

❧

Robert, now eighteen, is soon to be released from the boys' rehabilitation facility for juvenile delinquents where he has been since he was fourteen. He was placed there after he burned down a barn with more than twenty thoroughbred horses inside. Prior to that arson, he had been in juvenile court numerous times for assaults on animals and other children.

Robert's mother died when he was eight, and his life was spent moving from foster home to foster home. But he remembers that his mother, as she died, told him she wanted him to grow up to be a good person.

In deep trouble, the young man has been trying, with his counselor, to understand why he enjoys hurting things. She has helped Robert see that he is so numb from loss and moving from place to place, that only when he sees something in pain can he feel anything. Robert wants to feel and uses the pain of others to fulfill his desires.

Kim desired attention, and Mary Lee, special treatment. Neither wanted to hurt someone to fulfill her desires, but both did. Robert is like them and all of us who cannot forgive ourselves for transgressing. Robert hurt others to have what he wanted. But Robert is a threat to a larger number of people than Kim and Mary Lee are. If he and other evil transgressors are to forgive themselves or be encouraged to do so, he must confront the desire to injure others and, like all self-forgivers, demand of himself personal transformation.

When you decide how responsible you are for the event for which you must forgive yourself and a wrongdoing precipitated that event, you will learn more about your desires and your values. You will also understand the habits you have developed that allow you to violate right and wrong to get what you want. It is not pleasant to accept responsibility for cavalier hedonism, but if you are to forgive yourself, you must do just that and stop making excuses or blaming others.

Step 3: Uncover your secrets

Self-forgiveness is a process of confronting yourself without fear and carefully revisiting and reinspecting the circumstances of the harmful situation.

In Phase 1, you identified the nature of the unforgiven behavior. In Phase 2, you considered how, and if, you are accountable or if you've taken on unwarranted responsibility.

The third step in holding yourself responsible may be the most difficult part of the entire self-forgiveness process. At this juncture, the unforgiven examines even more closely his state of mind and unspoken thoughts and feelings at the time the incident took place.

Truthfulness gives people the power to make decisions. When a stockbroker tells a prospective buyer all the facts about the stocks he might purchase, the buyer is able to make her decision based on solid information. Facts are essential to self-forgiveness, too. If someone goes through the motions of forgiving himself for having bad judgment when he knows that real intent was to destroy another person's career, he is playing at self-forgiveness, not engaged in it. People who cannot forgive themselves are usually humbled by their own shortcomings; but to accept one's shortcomings or wrongdoings, self-deception must give way to bare and sometimes bitter truth.

Rachel has told herself and others that she cannot forgive herself because she made the wrong choice when she had to choose between two incompatible family obligations. She wanted to honor her moral duty to her mother; and at the same time, she wanted to be emotionally available to her daughter. Rachel tells herself that there was nothing else she could do. She struggles to forgive herself for choosing the wrong duty to attend to that night. Deep in her heart, though, Rachel knows there is more to the story. There is a secret something she can barely let herself see, let alone tell someone about. What Rachel really desired the night her mother died was a warm bubble bath, a glass of wine, and a quiet evening alone. She was angry at her mother, in fact, so angry with her for pulling at her IVs that she wished she were dead.

She was also angry at her brother and thought if her mother worsened during the night, it might scare him. Rachel alone knows how angry she really felt. She alone knows that she even hated her own daughter that night. She wanted to rest and drink wine and be left alone.

When people try to counsel or support Rachel (as when people try to comfort others who cannot forgive themselves when they appear to have done nothing wrong), Rachel cannot accept the support. She knows that if she were really honest, she would have to seek support for being angry, hateful, impatient, spiteful, and selfish. These things, Rachel believes, are beyond the support of other people. But if Rachel is to forgive herself, she will have to face the real truth of that night. Like Rachel, other people who cannot forgive themselves have had to choose between two duties or two obligations, but secrets, not choices, often make events unforgivable. The secrets that lie at the heart of an injury or wrongdoing may be the essence of non-forgiveness.

A soldier may be unable to forgive himself for killing women and children. He may tell his story over and over in group therapy and hear people persist in their view, "You couldn't have done anything else. Forgive yourself." What the soldier has not told anyone is that while he was killing civilians, he was sexually aroused. This is the secret at the heart of his non-forgiveness.

An incest victim, who continues into adulthood to hold herself responsible, after many years of counseling might still be unable to reveal that part of the experience felt good. Her body automatically responded, even when her mind viewed the act as deplorable. Because the woman cannot tell this to anyone, she cannot get to the heart of non-forgiveness: She cannot forgive herself for having anything other than feelings of hatred for her perpetrator and the acts perpetrated upon her.

Assumptions shattered by an unforgiven injury sometimes force people to see parts of themselves they can barely stand.

Desire is at the basis of wrongdoing and meanness; but the person who can forgive himself truly knows his own jealousy, envy, greed, pettiness, murderous heart, or mean thoughts. To forgive yourself, you will need to remove these parts of yourself from their secret hiding places and begin the process of really forgiving your *self*, not just what your choices were.

Summary

Phase 2, holding yourself responsible, involves analyzing your personal level of responsibility in the unforgiven situation. Clearing away the psychological debris—that is, the excuses and self-deception about your situation—is essential to forgiving. You will need to squarely face whether you might have known, or did know, the outcome of your actions. Even more essential is that you acknowledge any "evils" that you experienced at the time. Once you understand exactly what you are responsible for and then accept that responsibility, you can communicate it to another person and continue toward self-forgiveness.

Exercises for Phase 2: Holding Yourself Responsible

The exercises that follow are designed to help you decide if you were really responsible for the unforgiven situation. The first set of exercises will help you explore any complicating factors that might make it too easy to blame yourself or too likely to hold other people responsible for the things you do. The second set will help you assign the level of responsibility—from obviously responsible to doubtfully responsible. The third set is intended to help you acknowledge any unspoken secrets you may be hiding that make it impossible for you to forgive yourself.

You will probably want to complete the exercises in writing so that in the next phase of self-forgiveness (confession) you may share the exercises with another person if you choose.

SET 1: TO HELP YOU IDENTIFY ANY COMPLICATIONS TO ASSIGNING RESPONSIBILITY

When you were a child your family probably had its own patterns of assigning responsibility for its successes and failures.

Exercise 1: Success? Failure?

In the left-hand column of a piece of paper, write each family member's name. Next to each name, write one personal success that your family would all remember that person having.

EXAMPLE:

1. Mom
2. Dad
3. Me
4. Billy

Write down one personal failure for each person that the whole family would probably remember. Are some members without any personal successes or failures?

Exercise 2: Personal Success/Failure Story

1. Write what you recollect as your most successful experience as a child living at home. Next, describe how each family member responded to you.
2. Write what you consider to be your worst failure as a child living at home. Next, describe how each family member responded to you.

Exercise 3: Name That Family

The "Tough family" holds each member personally responsible for his or her successes or failures. In contrast, the "Angst family" never can understand why bad things happen to them. The Toughs assign responsibility to internal factors; whereas the Angsts assign responsibility to external or outside forces.

Can you make up a name for your family to describe the way your family behaved when a family member experienced troubles? Is there a name to describe your family when success comes to one of its members?

Exercise 4: The Scapegoat Search

When you think of your family, was any one member more wrong or more responsible for trouble than anyone else?

If so, who do you believe made you think this person was the "problem person"?

In retrospect, do you believe that assigning more responsibility to this person for trouble or failure was accurate?

Exercise 5: Internal or External?

1. In general, did your family assign its failures to external factors (luck, other people, fate, God) or to internal factors (hard work, character, tenacity, effort)? How did it assign its successes?
2. Can you see any influence your family's pattern has had over your experiences of success or failure?

Religion plays a major role in the way people understand the difficulties they face. Some people report that their religious beliefs make self-forgiveness easy. Others report that some of their beliefs had to be put aside so that they could finally forgive themselves.[25] (For example, the belief that one is innately bad has been rejected by some people.)

Exercise 6: Religion and Wrongness

Think about a childhood experience in which you suffered pain (from a death, or being hurt by a parent, or losing a friend).

Did you think that God had a role in your pain? How?

Exercise 7: Here and Now

Write an essay on the role God played in the situation you are unable to forgive yourself for. Try to write about God's role in causing the situation; in attempting to prevent the situation; in the feelings you have about yourself now.

Whether you are a man or woman has an impact on how you assign responsibility for your successes or failures. In the next exercises, examine your pattern of assigning responsibility.

Exercise 8: Patterns

Write down three of your major life successes. Underneath them, write three of your life's failures. Put a check mark under the appropriate set of sources for these successes or failures.

	SOURCE: PERSONAL CHARACTERISTICS (HARD WORK, TENACITY, STUPIDITY, TENDENCY TO GIVE UP, INTELLIGENCE, HUMOR)	SOURCE: OTHER PEOPLE, FATE, GOD, LUCK, EVIL SPIRITS
SUCCESSES		
1.		.
2.		
3.		

	SOURCE: PERSONAL CHARACTERISTICS (HARD WORK, TENACITY, STUPIDITY, TENDENCY TO GIVE UP, INTELLIGENCE, HUMOR)	SOURCE: OTHER PEOPLE, FATE, GOD, LUCK, EVIL SPIRITS
FAILURES		
1.		
2.		
3.		

Do you see any patterns? That is, do you attribute success to one type of source and failure to another?

The preceding exercises were designed to assist you in seeing if you have any complicating personal or family experiences that make it difficult to know who is responsible for what. If you have found a pattern of difficulties, you will want to discuss these with a friend, clergy, therapist, or support group. Tearing down any barriers to self-understanding is key to this second phase of self-forgiveness.

SET 2: TO HELP YOU ASSIGN LEVELS OF RESPONSIBILITY
TO YOURSELF FOR YOUR ACTIONS

Effort, foreseeability, and intentionality are key to accepting (or reject-
ing) whether you were responsible for your unforgiven injury. This set of
exercises is to be used when you are ready to determine how responsible
you were.

Exercise 9: The Did Know Exercise

Fill in the blanks with the words "could have known," "did know," or
"did not know."

When I (name the unforgiven situation), I (could have known) (did
know) (did not know) how much damage it would likely cause.

If you did know, you are probably responsible because you intended the
situation to happen, but hoped the results would not be so painful. If you
could have known or did not know, you did not expect the damage to be
as great as it was.

Exercise 10: Was It Necessary?

Write a story about the unforgiven experience where all the people
involved are the same except another person replaces you.

Would the same damage have happened without your involvement?

Exercise 11: Would Effort Have Helped?

You may ask yourself: If you had been aware of your limitation(s)
(involved in the unforgiven situation), would the situation have still
occurred?

Write down three ways you could have improved yourself enough
to have prevented the situation.

Do you think the situation might still have occurred?

Exercise 12: If I Am Responsible, Can Anyone Else Be?

Consistency refers to the idea that some people more consistently engage in wrongdoing over time than others. Even if all involved are corrupt, one of these people might have more consistently cheated (or lied, or stolen, etc.).

Answer these questions:

1. How many times did you engage in this behavior prior to this incident?
2. How many times before did someone find out?
3. How many times before were there painful repercussions?
4. Do you believe that your "mistake" was a part of a consistent personal pattern of behavior?
5. Could someone else be as responsible as you for causing this situation?

Exercise 13: How Difficult to Forgive?

Write down all the reasons you cannot forgive yourself. Which reason is the most honest? Why? Which characteristics of unforgiven incidences best describe yours?

SET 3: TO HELP YOU SORT THROUGH YOUR SECRETS

Some harm that people do to themselves or others may appear to outsiders to be less grave than it is to the person unable to forgive himself. You may have been told that you "did the best you could" or "simply followed orders" or were "too young to know better." You may not have been able to listen to other people's condolences because you knew something no one else knows about the situation. For example, you might have felt momentarily good about hurting someone, or physically aroused when assaulted, or angry at a person who died.

The final exercise in Phase 2 is to recollect the experience and write down your secrets.

Exercise 14: Secrets

If you know something about your unforgiven situation that is really at the heart of your inability to forgive yourself, write about it in as much detail as you can. Do not be afraid to remember and express parts of yourself that you think were, or are, unacceptable.

Put this exercise in a place of safekeeping. If you remember more details, return to the exercise and add them. You will return to this exercise on several occasions in the future.

Summary

In Phase 1, you were able to identify the nature of the unforgiven experience.

In Phase 2, you have found who is responsible and at what level.

With each phase of forgiving yourself, you come closer and closer to truth. Eventually, you will expose more of your truth to another person. For now, the hard work of confronting the unacceptable in yourself has taken you closer to the time when you can say, "I forgive myself."

CHAPTER 7

Confessing Your Flaws

As Kimberly headed, dejected, back to her camp cabin, she heard the distant crack of the bat behind her where the other kids were playing baseball. Only eight years old and not very athletic, she had, once again, not been chosen to play on the team. She fell, and the next thing she knew, she was lying in the ditch at the side of the road, her leg in excruciating pain. The girl crawled back up to the road and began to cry. She felt stupid for breaking her own leg and was embarrassed once again.

Mimi, one of Camp Arrowhead's most popular counselors, saw Kimberly crawling and immediately summoned the camp nurse. Kimberly was rushed by ambulance into town for X rays and to have a cast put on. There was much excitement in camp when the ambulance came and when Kimberly returned, too.

At camp headquarters, the Arrowhead camp director and all of Kimberly's counselors wanted to hear the girl's story. In the next hour, Kimberly told a series of lies for which she could not forgive herself for several years.

At first, Kimberly said someone had accidentally knocked her down and someone else had stepped on her. Pressed for details, she said a boy had pushed her down and twisted her leg. Pressed further to name the boy, Kimberly chose, at random, Johnny Taylor, a boy she barely knew. The rest of the summer, for Johnny, was miserable. He lost privileges at the swimming pool and waterfront. Other kids made fun of him, and Kimberly's cousin beat him up.

As summer ended, Kimberly felt small and dirty; but the little girl could find no way to make up for her lies. She was in too deep for that. However, Kimberly had learned an intriguing lesson. Her lies had worked. She felt bad, but had gotten much attention from the counselors and other kids. So, the next year, Kimberly identified another innocent boy for hurting smaller children on the playground. This boy was no longer allowed to go to recess; but again Kimberly lacked the courage to say she was wrong.

At nine years of age, Kimberly began to be worn down by her own guilty conscience. She was almost always ill; and she cried often, even though no adult could fathom the cause of the little girl's pain. Kimberly could not forgive herself. For years afterward, when she met someone from Camp Arrowhead, she asked them if they knew Johnny Taylor and if he was all right. At twenty-two, she still wonders about him.

Kimberly was being eaten by her guilt and her growing sense that she was becoming a person who used others to improve her own status. One day, she could stand it no more. She got out a piece of paper and wrote a letter of confession to her parents. She was terrified that they would punish her and, worse, regard her as a liar from then on. But her "constant remorse" was more painful than their response could possibly be.

Kimberly was lucky. She had confessed to people who did not condemn her. They were loving and gentle. Because of them, her healing could begin. They told her that many little girls lie and that they had suspected all along that she was burdened with lies. Kimberly had learned a profound lesson about forgiving—that telling others is essential to it. Kimberly explains:

> *"You have to really want self-forgiveness, and you have to know why. It comes with truth—when you are true to yourself and others [emphasis added]. It comes with pain because old wounds have to be opened and revealed—like picking off layers of skin covering an infection to let the pus drain out. . . Truth, courage, and the desire to move forward are one's tools. Self-forgiveness is one's reward."*

During Phase 2 of self-forgiveness, people look inward so that they can admit the nature of the damage they caused. In Phase 3, confessing your flaws, people must turn from themselves to other people. In this critical phase, people make their mistakes known to someone else. The third phase is an active phase that requires, as Kimberly wrote, truth, pain, revelation, courage, and the desire to move forward.

The word "confession" is quite different, really, from the word "admission." Some people may be able to admit their meanness or limitations and how responsible they were for causing damage to others or relationships, but they may not be able to confess what they have privately admitted. To admit something means to "accept [something] as true and valid."[26] Confession is more akin to the Latin word, *fateri*, meaning "to speak," instead of "to accept." A confession involves speaking to another person. An admission, by contrast, can be private, unspoken, and shared with only oneself. When you admit that your wrongdoing or meanness was responsible for an unforgiven injury, you have taken a major step; but when you confess this to another person, you have taken the first step that allows another person to invite you back in, just as Kimberly's parents did her. Until another person knows how alienated you are, you cannot be invited to rejoin your community.

Admissions reveal truths; confessions manifest these truths to others. During Phase 3, remember: *it is difficult to forgive yourself until you tell another person the harm you have done.*

Phase 3 of confessing your flaws requires three steps:

1. Recognize any previous experiences you may have had with confessing that may make it difficult to do again.
2. Select the right person or agent to whom you will confess.
3. Confess.

Each step takes a person closer to actually engaging in what might be the most humbling experience a person can undergo—letting someone else know just how flawed, mean, or wrong one really is underneath all the layers of camouflage used to conceal this from the eyes of others.

Step 1: Recognize any previous experiences with confessing that may now make confessing difficult

REPORTING VERSUS CONFESSION

Cindy hates the concept of confession. She hates it because she saw her father's pattern of confessing and abusing. When Cindy was about five, she first experienced her father's whip. He whipped her brother, too, sometimes to the point of bleeding. But when he whipped both children until they bled, there would follow several days of her father's tears and apologies. She realized many years later that her father was mentally ill, but Cindy, as a girl, only saw that her father's tears and apologies would escalate into full-blown self-hatred; and when his self-reproach reached fevered pitch, a "confession" was coming.

Cindy's father would dress especially for these "confessions." He would don his blue suit and head to the fundamentalist church that the family occasionally attended. Cindy and her brother can still barely talk about their memories of the look on their father's face when he returned from the church. They do remember, though, that he told them confession "cleansed the sinner and the sin." About a week after the "confession," their father would begin to beat them again. The cycle continued until Cindy was big enough to leave home.

Cindy learned that "confessing" was supposed to wipe a slate clean; but it also meant that nothing changed as a result of a confession. Cindy realized later that her father's idea of confession was wrong. Cindy's father was reporting his behavior to the minister, not confessing it. Confession is prompted by guilt, shame, remorse, and a deep desire to change. Reporting personal wrongdoings as flaws, by contrast, is prompted by a desire to be relieved of the burden of guilt and self-loathing. People who simply report their evil behaviors have no intention of changing. People who confess, however, are deeply committed to personal transformation.

RELIGION AND CONFESSION

Confessing may be difficult for you because of your religious upbringing. Some people carry great resentment from their childhoods, when they felt they were forced to conjure up things to confess to a priest to learn the habit of confession. When confession becomes a habit that is not accompanied with real feelings, people who have been expected to routinely engage in this ritual can come to resent its non-voluntary and insincere nature. If this has been your experience, you will need to remind yourself that, if you are to forgive yourself, your confession, in whatever form it takes and to whomever you direct it, must be real and from the heart, not a remnant of some involuntary ritual.

POORLY RECEIVED CONFESSIONS

You may have had the unfortunate experience of being punished for confessing.

⁂

When Sam was eleven, he stole some money from his father's billfold. He felt so bad he did not spend it. Instead, he ago-nized for three days whether to simply return it or confess to his father and hope his father would forgive him. Sam wanted to feel relief from his guilt, so he told his father about the money. His father was so angry at Sam that he took away the boy's privileges for a month, forbade the boy from speaking except when spoken to for two weeks, and called Sam's teacher to "warn" her. When Sam said, "I'm sorry, Dad, I'll never do it again," Sam's father said, "What good does sorry do now?" The boy was devastated. He never confessed to his father (or anyone else) again.

⁂

If this has been your experience, you will want, more than most people, to choose wisely the person to whom you speak about your most secret flaws and mistakes.

CONFESSION FOR FALSE RELIEF

Some people feel negatively about themselves, not because they are guilty of wrongdoing, but because (as described in Chapter 3), they experience constant shame, probably connected to low self-esteem. Celia was such a girl.

⁂

All her life, Celia felt badly about herself. She was shy and average. Her father was a doctor, her mother a prosecuting attorney, and her two older sisters outstanding students and athletes. Celia thought she was adopted.

In the fifth grade, Celia was ill much of the time, although her father found nothing physically wrong with her.

Celia just felt bad. One day in school, the girl's favorite teacher announced to the class that her dictionary had been taken and asked that the person who took it please return it. For some reason, Celia confessed to the teacher that she had taken the dictionary home even though she hadn't. After two days of confusion within her household and with her teacher, Celia confessed that her confession was not true. Her false confession to the teacher had made Celia feel good. For one of the few times she could remember, she did not feel bad about herself at all.

☙❧

Confessing became a habit with Celia. She knew many years later that she engaged in this behavior to reduce the terrible burden she felt about not being good enough to be a member of her family. She learned in therapy that, instead of doing something bad that she could really confess (like Kimberly), she had felt so bad about herself that she used false confession to get relief from her low sense of self-worth. Celia had tried to reduce her sense of worthlessness by falsely confessing wrongness; she believed confessing was a short-cut to a higher sense of self-esteem.

If you have used false confession to lift low self-worth, it is important that you recognize the difference between unforgiven injuries you have actually participated in and feelings of falling short. You may discover, for example, that one of your limitations contributed to an unfortunate situation, but hardly caused it.

When self-forgiveness is your goal, you will need to know what to confess and what has nothing to do with the damage you feel so badly about. Assessing your own habit of confessing will assist you in this.

TV "CONFESSIONS"

Another source of confusion about confessing is television. It is not uncommon today to turn on the TV at almost any time and witness public "confessions." Murderers speak to talk-show hosts from prison via monitor to confess the details of their murders. Daughters confess to mothers their affairs with the mothers' boyfriends. The litany goes on day after numbing day. Confessions to, and in front of, strangers are becoming commonplace; but they are also degrading the profound purpose of confessing, namely to reveal the private realm of one's life so that a person can fundamentally change the way she has lived.

> *Because [confessants] accept responsibility* and seek. . . assistance *[emphasis mine], they are in a position to offer some assurance of efforts to change: efforts great enough to affect their entire way of life, perhaps also to allow them to transcend their old selves and attain forgiveness or salvation in a future life. The change may be from deviance to normalcy, from wrong to right, from ignorance about the self to insight.*[27]

Confessants on television shows are not necessarily revealing the previously concealed so that they can change their lives. Although it may be a "near universal urge . . . to bare personal secrets,"[28] those who choose to confess on national television usually have motives other than exposing their flaws. The daughter on "Oprah" who confesses her affair with her mother's boyfriend can use the confession for darker purposes. A secret can mystify and tantalize, particularly if it is incompletely revealed. Most of us can immediately remember a friend whose partially shared secret made us want to know more. The daughter may, as a result of her revelation, feel special, lifted from the mundaneness of life. Her "confession" has changed her from being just a daughter to being a mysterious daughter; and many people value mysteries more than ordinariness.

Confessions can also be used as weapons. TV confessions are excellent examples of revealing secrets to cause harm. The mother is deeply wounded by her daughter's revelation; she is wounded publicly and placed in a situation in which she can neither hide nor defend herself. A secret can threaten like a knife held to the throat.

People who confess to strangers at bus stops or on national television may accomplish some other objective: the burden of secrecy may be lifted because it is shared. A secret-teller's mundane life might be temporarily heightened by "wickedness" revealed in the secret told. Even a person who listens to the "confession" of a total stranger in a city park may feel her day is more interesting as a result. The secret told to millions on "Oprah," like the secret told by a stranger in a park, may make listeners believe that they are somehow a part of "the Loop," where they are taken into an exclusive club called "Those Who Hear Confessions." But secrets revealed publicly are more like those of Cindy's father to his priest after he abused his children. They are merely reports of an activity that the "reporter" may have done, and have no objective other than to disclose that activity to someone else.

Public secrets in the form of "confessions" can be told to bring psychological relief to the teller, and to snare listeners into a trap where they believe that the "confessant" wants to change when he, in reality, does not. A listener can feel powerful because she was chosen to hear another person's most private thoughts, and the teller can continue his activities because the secret he told is not a confession, but a report instead. A public "confession" may misrepresent the profound nature of a genuine confession and, instead, provide a dangerous model for people who seek self-forgiveness and who need to confess to find it. Religion, families, social institutions, and television are all barriers that can obscure what a confession really is: a heartfelt sharing with another person to heal wounds and promote forgiveness.

Because confessing is essential to forgiving oneself, any barriers to confession must be removed. If you carry any confusion about confessing and its true purpose, this is the time to clear the confusion away.

Step 2: Select the right person to whom you will confess

A person confesses when the burden of the secrets she carries outweighs her fear of disclosing them. When this happens, the potential confessant must choose to whom she will confess. How does a person make this choice? What qualities should she look for? What pitfalls should be avoided?

Numerous thoughtful treatises have been written about confessing, but none is so useful for our purposes as the work of Sissela Bok in her book *Secrets*. In the chapter "Confessions," the author both instructs and warns about the darker sides of confessions and the people who listen to them.

People can confess to friends, acquaintances, strangers, or institutional experts who are trained to listen to people's secrets. Some listen better than others. Some are less dangerous than others; some are likely to be more helpful than others.

Confessions can be responded to with words of encouragement, ideas for making reparation, plans for purification rituals, requirements for penance, or simple non-judgment.[29] The sources of an unforgiven person's damage (that is, limitation, wrongdoing, or mistake) will probably determine which response the confessant needs. When a person is ready to confess, she is ready to embark on fundamental personal change. The one who hears a confession, then, should be both able and willing to help launch that change, whether the change is from wrong to right or from unawareness to insight. A confessant should "look for someone who can share one's burdens, interpret one's revelations, and show the path to release. . . ."[30]

Three Considerations for Confession
FAITHFULNESS

The bond between a person who confesses the secrets of her heart and the one who hears her is, if not sacred, forged from a special kind of faithfulness. The confessant must have faith that:

1. The listener will keep confidential what is confessed.
2. The listener will not use the secret to gain any personal advantage.
3. The listener will not condemn.

4. The listener will have a response that is comforting and/or give the confessant an idea about what to do next.

As stated earlier, the people to whom confessions are given are ordinarily friends, institutional listeners (usually experts such as psychotherapists or clergy), acquaintances, or strangers.

Faithfulness of Friends

Friends may listen without condemning. But friends, usually average people, may be able to give no more than comfort to a person confessing. Sometimes unconditional love may be all that is needed. Sometimes it is not.

If you choose a friend with whom to share your confession, choose wisely; friendships may have complications that make confessing very difficult.

Betsy, a dear friend of Camille's, "confessed" to Camille that she was having an affair with their mutual friend Samantha's husband. Betsy told Camille there was no one else she could trust with her secret. Betsy also asked Camille's advice on whether to break off the affair. Camille felt extreme guilt when Samantha came to her with a troubled heart and wept that she felt she was somehow failing her husband.

Camille, trying to be a good friend, has become part of a sticky web of secrecy. She is not sure if Betsy really wants to change, and she does not know how to advise her. She is not sure whether the "confession" was simply reporting, so she feels trapped and at a loss for solutions.

Friends can be rich sources of help when people are trying to forgive themselves. Their love is more than the objective support of professionals; but the limits can curtail true helpfulness, especially if the confession becomes too complex. What does a friend do if, for example, someone confesses to child abuse or a hit-and-run accident? There are no formal ethical codes to govern whether friends must report these incidents. Friends can soon find themselves "in over their heads" if a confession has serious overtones.

Lila felt guilty for more than thirty years about her deep hatred for her father. When she could not bear the guilt of what she considered her "sin" any longer, she confessed the hatred to her friend, Martha:

> *"Martha. . . told me over and over, 'God loves you. You are a beautiful person. . . .' I was able to share anything with her, and she still responded with love. When I was finally able to say those hateful words out loud and not be condemned for it, and not think I was absolutely terrible, I felt a weight lift off. Until I told her I hated my own father, I felt stuffed up.*

Friends are among life's greatest assets. If unconditional love is all you need in response to what you want to confess, a friend may be exactly the right person to turn to.

Clergy

Clergy may also listen without judgment, and unlike most friends, they have the capacity to help determine an appropriate penance for your "sin." Clergy can offer rituals of purification. A clergyperson, unlike a friend, though, may not love you unconditionally, and may also be duty-bound to report your confession, should the confession contain "threats against the public good or against an innocent third person."[31]

Clergy, for many Christians, are the first choice when they decide they must confess.

Sue, despite her lifelong Catholic upbringing, chose to have an abortion:

> *"I grew up during a time when the Catholic Church had lists of moral and venial sins and put young children into dark confessional boxes when they were seven years old. I went to*

Catholic grade school . . . and ended up teaching in Catholic elementary schools for over fifteen years. . . .

"I felt both love and hate toward the man with whom I got pregnant. He was the one I married . . . [but] I loved myself enough to want a better life for myself. I hated myself for having killed my child—or at least a potential *child.*

"I went to a priest when I was thinking about divorcing. The priest told me I had suffered enough. He told me to stop punishing myself. He told me God had forgiven me a long time ago. It's taken me about a decade to start believing what he said.

"Th[at] one priest undid all the damage done by scores of others who had put into a small child notions of a God who would condemn his children to the eternal fires of hell."

Professionals

"Professional helpers" presumably are trained to listen to their clients without condemning them, and they are bound by legal and ethical rules of confidentiality. Confidentiality is a reassurance to most clients, but there are limits to it. Also, there are vast differences among professionals about confidentiality. A confessant can weave a sticky web around the one who hears; but the listener can, if she is not competent, use the other person's private revelations to measure her own professional "talents" and enhance her own sense of self-esteem.

Ned sought help from Nancy, a young psychotherapist. Ned wanted to confess that he was trying to end a year-long affair with a local minister's wife. Not used to psychotherapy or psychotherapists, Ned did not know whether Nancy's rather constant insistence that he "tell all" and be "totally honest" was ordinary or simply Nancy's personal style.

After several weeks of intense therapy, Ned still had not revealed the name of the woman, wanting to protect her and fearing any fallout that might come should anyone find out.

Not satisfied without knowing, Nancy probed more deeply each session for the name. Truthfulness, she insisted, was essential to "healing."

Ned could not have known that Nancy measured her own effectiveness by how many secrets she could entice a client to reveal. If a client said, "I've never told anyone this before," Nancy secretly congratulated herself for how good a therapist she was becoming. To Nancy, there was a direct relationship between the number of client confessions and her own competence—so much so that she felt herself losing interest in clients who seemed to have no secrets.

Ned felt Nancy's subtle pressures. He saw her facial expressions soften when he revealed something new. Desperate for help and becoming dependent on Nancy, Ned told her the woman's name.

Ned also could not have known that Nancy talked about her clients with her husband over dinner—to "process" the day. Nancy revealed Ned's secrets to her husband who happened to be a longtime member of the church board of directors. Nancy's husband called another board member and reported that the minister's wife was having an affair. He did this, he said, for the good of the church community, whose well-being was more important than the well-being of the minister, his wife, or Nancy's client.

Soon, Ned's secret was known widely. His marriage was coming unglued; and the minister and his wife were facing forced resignation. Ned never knew that Nancy had shared his confession. In fact, he saw Nancy for another two years to help him through his divorce.

❧❦

Professional helpers vary in their fidelity to clients in the same manner that friends do. When you come to the point of sharing your unforgiven injury with someone else, ask yourself some questions:

What reason does the listener have to keep my secret to herself?

What reason might the listener have to share my secret with another person?

Would I feel uncomfortable asking the listener directly if she will protect my privacy and keep my confession confidential?

Would the secrets I am about to share put the listener in over her head?

What kinds of information in a confession must the listener report to authorities?

Hearing another person's intimate and troubling stories and not using these stories to one's own advantage is really part of the essence of true friendship or true professionalism. Evaluate your choice of a potential listener very carefully. Recall whether your friend has told you intimate details about anyone else's life that you feared were shared in confidence. Ask questions of professionals. Talk to other people about the reputation of any professional you might be considering. Try to recall if you know of anyone who left your church after a divorce or other personal tragedy, and you were told that clergy or church members had disapproved of these members' behavior.

When you think about confessing, consider what you would do or how you would feel if others discovered your situation (presuming they didn't know already). If it is harder to live with your secret than it might be to have others know about it, then you will want to carefully go ahead with confessing. Remember, though, that you are in control, not only over choosing to whom you will confess, but also how fast and in how much detail. Beware of people who want to know more, or more quickly, than you are prepared to tell them.

THE CONTENT OF YOUR CONFESSION

The content of what you want to confess can help you make your decision about the best person with whom to share your troubled heart. When you confess your unforgiven situation to another person, you will be sharing with that person a wrongdoing, a limitation, a mistake, or an act of meanness that damaged or destroyed someone else and/or your relationship with that person.

In Phase 2, you might have been able to judge how grave your unforgiven act was in relation to other injuries that hurt people. A limitation, such as having a "blind spot" about your capacity to help your child, cannot be as grave as an act of intentionally maiming another person. The person whose fundamental transformation during self-forgiveness will be from being "blind" about herself to being insightful is vastly different from the person who wants to change from being a wrongdoer or mean person to being moral or kind. The content of confessions will be as different as the pathways to transformation.

In general, the closer the content is to a mistake or limitation, the more likely a confessant can choose someone who does not condemn and who can show a person how to overcome her flaws and see through her defenses. By contrast, the closer the content of a confession is to a wrongdoing or an evil wrongdoing, the more likely a confessant will seek out a person who can offer penance or purification.[32]

Bertha sat in women's prison for six years, convicted of involuntary manslaughter, before she could admit that she slashed her girlfriend's wrists during a fight over cocaine. With the help of the prison chaplain and her Narcotics Anonymous group, Bertha admitted that she not only took her friend's life, but that she had hurt other people along the way. Now she is truly sorry. She hates herself and wants to make things right. She also knows that when she killed her friend, she looked directly into her friend's frightened, confused, and pleading eyes and said, "Die, bitch." No one else knows this, but the words echo through Bertha's mind and make her feel that she is dying.

Bertha wants, almost desperately, to confess. She wants relief from her secret. She also wants to contact her friend's family to see if she can somehow do something for them; and

Bertha wants to accept an additional penance. This she thinks she can do only through the chaplain.

As her need to confess becomes stronger, she fears that the chaplain might let prison officials know that she had murderous intent in her heart when her friend died. And she fears that they would retry her and increase her sentence, so Bertha decides to confess to God.

In the quiet of the chapel, the prisoner drops to her knees and tells God what she had said to her friend as she died. She whispers the words of "Amazing Grace" and awaits God's forgiveness. At the end of the hour, she feels relieved, but not cleansed. Bertha is now considering contacting her own home minister so that he could hear her words—this time spoken aloud.

For some, confessing directly to God opens the door to forgiveness and, therefore, to self-forgiveness. God's hearing a confession may not result in immediately felt grace; but confessing to another person also does not result in immediate forgiveness. Confessions open the door to change, transformation, and forgiveness—they do not simply confer these profound concepts onto people who confess.

Bertha ultimately decided not to confess to another person. She feared not only legal repercussions, but she also believed that another person could offer her little help in transforming her life. Her confession would stay with God, and her ideas about restitution and penance for involuntary manslaughter would come from clergy, friends, and her Narcotics Anonymous group. Her confession to God opened the door to change. With the help of God and others, she has decided to begin her transformation without confessing to another person.

EXPECTATIONS

Confession versus Apology

A third factor to consider when you decide to whom you will confess is your expectation. What do you want to happen as a result, and how likely is it that you will get what you want? At the very least, most people who truly confess something personal, difficult, and secret want:

1. To share their burden
2. To face no condemnation
3. To open the door to personal change

Some people may have additional expectations, however. Some may expect that a confession will erase guilt. Confessions may open the door to re-creating the self and ultimately reducing guilt; but in all probability, bad feelings in general (regret, shame, and so on) will remain firmly in place for some time to come.

A person's expectations of what will result from a confession may help determine to whom to confess in very limited but important ways: If your expectation is that confession opens up the possibility of a dialog with God, the person you choose should be in a position to increase the likelihood of this dialog. If your expectations are that you will participate in a ritual of purification, then you will want to seek out a person who is open to, or who performs, these kinds of rituals.* Finally, some people who need to forgive themselves consider going directly to the person they hurt to confess. They expect that a confession might mend their relationship. These people should be aware of the difference between a confession and an apology. Confessions are often followed by apologies,

---

*Rituals of purification are, in the Western context, probably most often performed by clergy; but American Indian groups, healing groups, other religious sects, and some psychologists also engage in group rituals of cleansing and purification.

at least when confessions are made to the people or person one has hurt. But confessions are *not the same* as apologies. A confession reveals a secret. An apology sets off a dialog between an injurer and the person she harmed. Oftentimes, the content of a confession and the content of an apology are vastly different—and should be so.

⇝⇜

Buddy, an aging jock, challenged his lifelong friend, Bob, at the company Fourth of July picnic to swim across a river. Bob refused even though he was a good swimmer. He had been on the high school swim team and, years ago, had won numerous medals. (In fact, Bob was still considered a community hero for winning the state boys' swimming meet.) Bob refused Buddy's challenge because he knew that neither man had swum much in the last couple of years; but when Buddy continued to provoke him, he gave in. The two old friends jumped into the river. Halfway across Buddy began to sputter. Bob heard it, but he was not aware that his friend was drowning.

After several more minutes, Bob lifted his head out of the water to see Buddy being dragged downstream by the current. He managed to swim hard enough to grab Buddy's arm, but was not strong enough to hang on. Buddy's body was found later that afternoon.

Bob was stricken with grief and shame; the whole community saw that he could no longer swim well enough to save his friend. A day or so later, someone told him in confidence that Buddy had been drinking heavily late into the night before the picnic. When he found this out, Bob was furious. Not only did his friend provoke him into doing something unwise that exposed his limitations to the entire community, he also put Bob in a dangerous position of trying to save a swimmer who was probably still intoxicated and could not save himself because of it. Bob privately believes that Buddy got what he deserved. He let himself go physically. He drank too much, and he was cavalier with his friends and family. For these feelings, Bob cannot forgive himself—not for being unable to save his friend.

꒰꒱

Bob, who only now can admit to himself that he was angry with Buddy when he let go of him in the rushing waters, wants to apologize to Buddy's wife for not having the strength to hang on. But Bob may not want to confess to her. His angry thoughts about Buddy would only hurt her. Bob might confess his thoughts to a therapist or cleric to find relief for his sense of shame, but to Buddy's wife, he will only apologize.

If a person expects that a confession will clear the way for an apology and possible reaffirmation of the relationship, she should consider quite carefully the content of her confession and whether the secret told might do more harm than good.

Kimberly, whose story began this chapter, always wanted to confess to the boy whose summer she ruined. Had she been able to find him, though, her confession might have done little to reduce her bad feelings about herself. The boy would probably have been so taken aback by the revelation that, unless he were a most unusual person, he would not have, at least immediately, forgiven her.

Confessions open doors. They do not allow people to come back into the house. They allow for the possibility of apologies, but they are not apologies. They point the way toward transforming one's life, but they do not transform people.

When you choose the person to whom you will confess, then, choose someone who will listen without condemning you. Choose someone who will not use your secret to bolster her own ego or to entertain other people. Choose someone who can offer support, if support is all you need, and the hope of finding a method of transforming yourself, if you are ready for that undertaking. Above all, know that a confession alone will not take away your regret or result in "instantaneous grace" or forgiveness from the one you hurt.

Confession goes beyond admission because when you confess, the words that fall from your lips will reach someone else's ears. Make sure that those ears are open to hear you and to give you some relief.

Step 3: Confess

A confession could be spoken or written, planned or spontaneous. When people have difficulty deciding exactly how to confess, it may be that their mistakes or wrongdoings seem at times very clear and intelligible, but at other times, obscure and at odds with their everyday life. If this is your situation, you may choose to write out a confession.

Writing a confession gives a person the opportunity to relive her experiences so that they seem more real. Writing tears down the defenses against the tendencies most people have to put their uncomfortable life experiences "on the back burner." A written confession gives a person time to let an injury become consistent in the way it is experienced, particularly when it has taken the confessant a long time to decide how responsible she really was. Written confessions provide a person who lacks the courage to reveal her wickedness to people face-to-face a medium for self-exposure. Kimberly's written confession to her parents is an example.

Kimberly confessed to her parents that she had purposely iden-
tified an innocent boy as the person who broke her leg. She told
them how guilty and ashamed she felt. She shared her fear that
she was a person who lied too easily, and she asked their for-
giveness. Kimberly could not have said those things to her par-
ents, but she could put them down on paper.

A written confession may seem innocent enough at the time it is written but, in truth, a person cannot know where written materials end up. If your written confession is put into a therapist's file, for instance, it can be inspected by state mental health officials, subpoenaed by a court, or seen by other clinic personnel (therapists or typists). Some things told to a therapist are required by law to be shared with authorities (for example, previous sexual assault of a child). Some therapists may believe that if the safety and well-being of another is endangered, they are ethically bound to report the matter to authorities. For example, if an AIDS victim confesses having frequent unprotected sex with unsuspecting partners, his therapist might report this, even though it was told in confidence.

A confession does not necessarily mean that no punishment will follow. If you write your confession, ask your therapist (clergyperson or friend) where it will be placed. It is safest to assume that your written confession may be read by others at some time. It is common for therapists to reveal private information of clients who die. Many books, even best-sellers, are written using client case files when clients did not consent to the release of the files prior to their deaths—a questionable practice.

People may want to write their confessions out so that they can come to accept themselves; but they probably should destroy the written confession and simply confess verbally.

VERBAL CONFESSIONS

Once you have chosen the person to whom you will confess, select a time and place for the confession. You might want to tell a professional that you are going to reveal something important. A professional can then describe the limits to confidentiality that she adheres to—that is, what kinds of information she reveals to authorities or seeks consultation with other professionals about.

Confessions, regardless to whom they are spoken, should be complete. If people reveal only partial information, the support and comfort they may receive from the listener can seem false and hollow. If the Vietnam war veteran, for example, continues to report that he murdered civilians, he might receive comfort from others for following orders, but not for the secret for which he really loathes himself.

A confession humbles. It takes away any false pride that has prevented a person from trying to accept the fact, not only that human beings can be ugly, but that she has been an ugly human being. In a sense, when a person decides to confess, the decision leads to one of life's most profound experiences. One human being brings to another evidence of how base and ugly the human species can be. The other responds with love. A confession is a moment that expresses complete humanness—human vulgarity confronting human compassion. In this sense, the opportunity to confess is the invitation of a lifetime, an invitation to see, firsthand, the full spectrum of what we are capable of, the capacity to hurt and the capacity to love. Choose the one to whom you confess wisely.

In summary, the third phase of self-forgiveness, confessing your flaws, is essential to being able to forgive yourself. When you can reveal your secrets, you begin to transform your life.

Exercises for Phase 3

Confessing to another person is one of life's most interesting invitations. You are invited to remove the weight of the camouflage you carry. To do this, you should first clear away any barriers to confession that stand between you and the experience. Then you should choose wisely to whom you will confess. Finally, you can decide what form your confession will take.

The following three sets of exercises correspond with the three steps of Phase 3: recognize barriers; decide to whom you will confess; and confess. Each set will help you move closer toward full disclosure of your humanness.

SET 1: RECOGNIZE PREVIOUS EXPERIENCES THAT MIGHT
MAKE CONFESSING DIFFICULT

Confessing and reporting are not synonymous. Confessing signals that
people are ready to change; reporting does not. If you have experienced
situations where someone close to you used the word "confess" inaccurately, try this next exercise.

Exercise 1: Confession?

Try to remember anyone in your family who "confessed" frequently.
These confessions may have been at twelve-step meetings, church,
among friends, or to a family member.

1. What do you think the purpose of the confessions really was?
2. Were the "confessions" honest?
3. Were the "confessions" followed by behavior changes?
4. Do you think the confessant really felt guilty?

People can share their secrets to trap other people into pledges of silence.
Has another person's "confession" ever put you in an uncomfortable
situation?

Exercise 2: Confessing as a Trap

Can you recall anyone confessing or sharing a secret with you that
became a trap for you? Write about this incident. What were the motives
of the confessant?

Did the confession signal the confessant's determination to change
his or her ways? How, if in any way, did this experience influence your
ideas about confessing your secrets to other people?

Some people, especially children, have the sad experience of feeling
truly contrite and then confessing to someone who subsequently
condemns or unjustly punishes them.

Exercise 3: Dangerous Confession?
Did you ever confess and regret it?

1. Write a detailed account of the incident.
2. Tell someone else about the incident.
3. List at least two ways the experience might have affected your current attitudes toward confessing.

Think about any experiences you have had with confession. Have they been associated with church, your family, school? You probably have some positive experiences with confession and some negative, depending upon where you confessed and to whom.

Exercise 4: The Positive/the Negative

1. What confession brought you the most relief? Why?
2. What confession hurt you the most? Why?
3. From what group was the person to whom you confessed (i.e., family, church, school)?

Do you recognize any patterns about your willingness to confess to a member of your family, church, and so on, that might be a result of the positive and negative experiences you had earlier in your life?

Exercise 5: Compulsive Confession
Was there ever a time in your life when you felt an overwhelming need to confess? Write about that time. How old were you? What had you done? To whom did you want to confess?

Looking back, can you see any particular reasons for this behavior (for example, to please a priest, to be validated by a parent, to be reassured by an important adult)?

Are there any lingering remnants of your need to confess that might make you feel responsible for causing something bad to happen when you are not really responsible at all?

SET 2: SELECTING THE RIGHT PERSON TO WHOM YOU
WILL CONFESS

The second set of exercises is designed to help you decide to whom you
will confess. Because this decision is so important, it should be made with
great care.

Exercise 6: Trust

If you are thinking of confessing to your clergyperson or therapist, complete this exercise.

At your next session or meeting, ask the clergy or therapist the
following questions:

1. What information are you legally required to report to any
   authority?
2. Is there any particular client problem that you often consult another
   professional about?
3. Would you tell me if you talked to someone else about my situation?
4. Who can read my files?
5. Have you ever shared any information about me with someone else?

A competent professional or clergyperson should be able to answer
your questions without being angry or defensive. If you are not satisfied
with the answers, consider confessing to another person or, possibly,
changing therapists.

You will decide ahead of time what you hope to gain from
confessing. There are a number of possibilities. Are your expectations
reasonable?

Exercise 7: Reasonable Expectations

Below is a list of positive results people hope to gain when they confess
something personal and difficult. To the right of the list, write in the
name of the person or persons who might be able to provide the results
you would like.

GAINS	NAMES
1. Acceptance	1.
2. Restitution	2.
3. Penance	3.
4. An ally to see me through this	4.
5. Relief from guilt	5.
6. Immediate forgiveness	6.
7. Unconditional love	7.
8. Ideas for how I may change	8.
9. A ritual that might help purify me	9.
10. Reassurance that I am okay	10.

Exercise 8: A Second Opinion

After you have decided to whom you will confess, answer these questions:

1. Has anyone ever told you about an instance where the potential listener broke a requirement of confidentiality?
2. Have you ever heard the potential listener discuss a private matter of another person when it was unlikely that the third party was aware of the discussion?

If any information indicates to you that the potential listener is unreliable where confidentiality is concerned, you may want to consider another person.

SET 3: CONFESSING

When you confess, you may want to write everything down over time so that you leave out nothing that you want to tell someone.

Exercise 9: Writing a Confession

Over the course of one week, write down what you want to confess. Return to the confession during the week to add to it or change inaccurate portions. If it helps you to see the situation more clearly, include your level of responsibility and any remaining secrets you have, as yet, told no one. Keep this in a safe place until you are ready to share it.

The conclusion of the third phase of forgiving yourself is to confess your mistakes to another person.

Exercise 10: Confessing Your Flaws

Make an appointment with the friend or professional to whom you want to confess. Tell yourself that the burden of self-doubt you carry will be lighter once you share your secret.

Include everything you want to tell someone else, but do not feel that you must tell more than you want or are ready to.

Confessing your secret can be an overwhelming and emotional moment. A confession "may bring . . . the chance to re-create oneself . . . by making manifest 'all that is secret and hidden,' confession brings sin into the light."[33] If you have been brave enough to come this far in your work toward self-forgiveness, you can go the rest of the way. As humbling as confessing may be, confession allows you to come face-to-face with the best aspects of humanity—unconditional love, compassion, and hopefulness. Few other life situations provide such a rare opportunity.

Transformation

Maria was twenty-two and pregnant with her first child. She was excited that she would soon become a mother. All through her pregnancy she had eaten right, had not drunk alcohol or smoked, and had gotten good prenatal care. Five weeks before she was to deliver, her water broke. She called her doctor, but he was on vacation.

Maria's husband rushed her to the emergency room. The first doctor they saw advised that labor be induced, but because he was going off duty, he did not press his point. A second doctor came in soon after and advised Maria and her husband to wait a while, maybe three days, before inducing labor. Later that day, a third doctor suggested waiting as long as possible.

Maria waited.

Three days later, the young woman became septic. Labor was induced, and a very sick baby was rushed forty miles away to a clinic where he died.

Maria could not forgive herself for her child's death. For five years, she believed she should have done something, known better. She believed that good mothers protect their children. She felt stupid, worthless, and angry.

After two years of grief and self-loathing, Maria demanded to see the hospital records. Legal battles ensued; Maria finally saw the records. As she feared, they revealed tragic medical negligence, confusion among hospital staff, and the totally unnecessary death of her perfectly treatable infant.

Maria sued the hospital, and Maria won.

Today, she is a changed person, a wiser person. Her assumptions about herself and the world have given way to a new perspective on life. Maria now accepts that people are flawed. She understands that tragedies occur. And she knows that some things happen despite all of a person's careful attempts to prevent harm or hard work to make sure that life goes well.

Maria is content with her life; and she knows that much of what is to come lies outside her control.

⋙⋘

Transformation is the subject matter of countless novels, treatises, movies, and textbooks. In a sense, philosophy, psychology, and theology all address the essential nature of human beings and how, or if, a human being can change fundamentally. Transformation is not simply change; transformation is fundamental and essential change. When people are transformed, they re-create themselves.

Transformation following an injury in which a person damages himself, another person, or a relationship, is very similar to the transformation, or "mini conversions," that a person who is damaged by another person goes through. A person who finally can forgive someone else for an injury changes from:

1. A person who does not understand the harm done to him to someone who incorporates his injury into his life and no longer considers himself injured

2. A person who blames himself to someone who blames another to one who blames no one

3. A person who does not want to change to someone who accepts that he must change to one who directs the course of his change
4. A person who wants the present to return to the past to someone who hangs on to the present to one who looks only to the future
5. A person who is acted upon to someone who cannot act to one who acts on the things he knows he can act on
6. A person who trusts to someone who does not trust to one who may choose to trust if he wants
7. A person who loves to someone who hates to someone who either loves in a different way or is indifferent to the injurer
8. A person who feels equal in power or resources to someone who feels depleted of resources to one who feels equal again[34]

By contrast, a person who finally can forgive himself changes from:

1. A person who struggles to admit his mistakes, limitations, or wrong-doings to someone who has gained insight into his flaws to one who understands that everyone is flawed
2. A person who hates or feels guilty about himself to someone who regrets what has happened to one who uses what has happened to set his life on a new course
3. A person who may not know of his flaws to someone who can admit them to himself to one who can confess them to others
4. A person who was not fully aware of his connectedness to others or spirituality to someone disconnected from others or spirituality to one who is again connected to one or both

Transformation requires intensive effort and a continuing undiluted confrontation with truth. A person who has admitted his failure, held himself responsible for it, and confessed it is poised on the threshold of the final act: seeking readmission to the human community.

In Phase 4, it is important to know that *you cannot forgive yourself until you commit yourself to personal change.*

Types and Methods of Transformation

Transformation can mean complete reformation of one's life—for example, reformation of what a person believes, how he lives, with whom he spends his time, and how he works and plays. Or transformation can be a term used to apply to one emotion or experience. In the heat of an argument, for instance, rage can be transformed into laughter.

Some people who forgive totally re-create themselves. Others re-create parts of their emotional lives, or life goals, or ways of dealing with people. In other words, some parts of their beliefs and ways of life are transformed; but they are not transformed. Is the person who forgives himself and who is totally transformed more worthy in some important way than a person who forgives himself and has changed less fundamentally? Should one forgive himself more easily than the other? No. Both are worthy of self-forgiveness. They have sought different methods of reconnecting with others.

Two people may select different pathways to self-forgiveness, but both still regret the damage they have caused. "Born again" or simply wiser, a person who forgives himself does not forget the regret of his past.

Three different pathways to transformation make it possible for a person to be reunited with the human or spiritual community:

1. Using coping strategies that reconnect people
2. Transforming one's basic life assumptions
3. Engaging in purification rituals that reconnect people with other people and spiritual activities

Some people who finally forgive themselves take all three pathways; some take only one. No one pathway is more noble than another. Maria, for example, chose the first pathway to transformation. She marshaled all the coping strategies she could to help her transcend her situation. Once she did that, her assumptions about life and people quietly and fundamentally changed.

COPING STRATEGIES THAT TRANSFORM PEOPLE

Coping strategies used by people to confront life's stressful situations are cited in psychological literature under five labels:

1. Social comparison
2. Assessing benefits
3. Emotional-focused
4. Appraisal-focused
5. Problem-focused

These approaches to coping are commonly described strategies people are said to use to reduce stress in their lives.[35] Some of these strategies are particularly pertinent to the process of self-forgiveness.

Social Comparison

People use social comparisons to assess how well or badly they are doing in life. For example, a person who gets a raise may compare his raise to that of another person at his workplace to see how he is "stacking up." If the worker is angry and hurt that his raise is smaller than he had anticipated, he might feel better if a coworker gets a smaller raise than he did. If he discovers that his coworker got a bigger raise, he might experience more anger and stress. People cope with all sorts of life events by engaging in social comparisons, including events in which others may be hurt because of them.

When a person feels badly about himself, he seeks "self-enhancement." When people are hurting, in other words, they may compare themselves to people who are even worse off.[36] A "downward social comparison" can make a person feel better and help him accept his situation with greater ease.

Candace, who stole money from Ted, her boss, compared herself to others in her family. Using this strategy, she decided that she was far better off than some of her family members.

"When I looked at my family and what other people had done,
I realized I wasn't the only one to commit wrong. And it wasn't
the end of the world. My brother screwed around on his wife
and now doesn't have her or a house. His kids can't stand him.
My father left us when we were little and didn't realize until
years later how it hurt him.

"I have a job. I have my daughter. My grandparents still
love me, even though I know how hurt they are. In a way, I'm
much better off than my brother or dad.

"I learned enough to know that you can do things that
you're sorry for and then try to make it right before it ruins you.
But you can't go back and change it. You can try to hold the
wrong you did against somebody else, or learn to live with it. If
you blame someone else, you miss out on a lot of love. Every-
one's human; everybody makes mistakes. I've made plenty of
them, but I'm better off than lots of people."

Once Candace compared herself to others, she concluded that she is
relatively "lucky." The "not so lucky" never admit they are wrong or
apologize. Their lives are on hold. Hers is moving forward. Candace put
it this way: "Don't be too hard on yourself. Life goes on if you let it."
Comparing herself to others who cannot forgive themselves, Candace
believes her life is back on track.

Benefit Analysis

This strategy is used by people who have both been hurt and hurt others.
Like people who forgive unforgivable injuries or who are able to cope
well with traumatic victimization, people who can forgive themselves
find some "higher good" or benefit resulting from their tragic experience.[37] These benefits may be in lessons they have learned, people they
have met, struggles they no longer have, or even activities they can now
engage in that were previously too difficult to attempt. Lena could forgive herself after she was able to transform her wounds into assets.

Lena, at late middle age, struggled to forgive herself for putting both parents into nursing homes. She could care for neither; she had to work and had no siblings to help.

> *"I'm stronger spiritually. I'm becoming more patient. I can be of help to others because of having experienced the loss you feel when you can no longer help a parent, but the parent isn't dead.*
>
> *"I went through a period when I questioned God. But now I know; times of trial make us stronger, and I know God never leaves us.*
>
> *"I've also started going to a support group, and I realize this is life. We have to make decisions. I'm not alone—others in the group have faced the same situation I have."*

Lena will always regret that she had to make such a hard decision and feel sad that her parents became so feeble; but she can now step back into life. From her experience, she can now help others. She has made friends; and she knows that she did the best she could. Her relationship with God was strengthened as a result of her difficulties. Lena used the experience as a lesson from which to learn.

Some people who hurt others, or are hurt by them, reframe the experience so that it becomes their greatest personal asset: a resolve they use to help others avoid the mistakes they have made or that helps others not to be so hard on themselves.[38] Murderers in prison may devote their lives to speaking to teenage first offenders; drunk drivers may go into schools to preach against drinking and driving. These may be symbolic forms of restitution (see next section), but the resulting feelings and experiences of being reconnected with people are the paradoxical gifts flowing from such damage. Maria, whose abortion caused her so much pain and who felt so injured by the Catholic Church, altered her life completely. She has become a practicing minister who speaks often about forgiveness and the "Grace Fullness" of God. Her experience became her life's work.

Appraisal-focused, Emotion-focused, and Problem-focused Coping Strategies

People use three other coping strategies to transform stressful events into opportunities for self-forgiveness. When people cope effectively, they do not simply lie back and let life and emotion happen to them. People who cope effectively are in the constant process of actively constructing their own emotional lives.

To compare the three strategies, a person using an appraisal-focused strategy to reduce a stressful situation might try to redefine the situation as a challenge or opportunity rather than a threat. A person using a problem-focused approach to reduce stress tries to define the situation as a problem that can be solved. Someone using an emotion-focused strategy to reduce stress might try to dampen or suppress negative thinking related to the stressful situation. This last strategy is least useful when people are attempting to forgive themselves because, although a guilty or ashamed person cannot and should not want to experience these feelings in full force or all the time, self-forgiveness (like regret) "depend[s] on the ability and willingness to call up and to experience the emotional aspects . . . as fully as possible."[39]

Dampening emotions can delay self-forgiveness and hurt people over time. Donald's experience is a case in point. He is a middle-aged college professor who wrote about his experience of self-forgiveness that came unexpectedly and was finished, as far as he wanted it to go, during the course of one weekend.

🌿

"I am a Vietnam vet. I came home uninjured. I left behind the thirty-five men in my platoon for whom I had been responsible. We all exchanged names and addresses and promises of contact. None of us has contacted each other . . . . I did not hold

myself accountable until years after when I finally realized the sense of guilt I felt for abandoning the men who trusted me.

"I closed the door on the experience for almost twenty years and could not see how the experience had affected the person I had become. The major source of difficulty came from emotional foreclosure by me.

"Shortly after reading a book on Post Traumatic Stress Disorder, I attended a weekend church leadership conference focusing on personal spiritual growth. During the conference, with God's grace, I was able to see the need for self-forgiveness and recognize the guilt I carried. [I was then able] to turn it over to God.

"It was all that simple, but not painless, because the guilt and pain [I felt] created many problems in my life. [Now I am] freed from a burden that was killing me."

Emotional dampening only postpones self-forgiveness. It does not erase the unforgiven event from memory. People need to experience their mistakes in order to forgive themselves for them.

A problem-focused coping strategy may be the most effective for people who are trying to forgive themselves. A problem-solver, compared to a person who uses emotion-focused or appraisal-focused coping strategies, defines his problem, generates solutions, assesses the alternative solutions for their effectiveness, and then acts.[40]

There are at least two (and probably more) strategies that a person using a problem-focused approach can use that will reconnect him with people he harmed or with other people who might reassure him or support him: apologies and restitution. Both are effective solutions to opening up sealed-off relationships, and both can be delivered directly to the person harmed or, indirectly, to others who act as "stand-ins" for the people who were actually injured.

Apologies

As the newspaper cartoon character Eli opined in *For Better or For Worse*, "An apology is the super glue of life. It can repair just about anything." It is true that apologies can repair much; but in a life-altering experience that does such damage as to break relationships, apologies may or may not repair them. They can, however, reconnect people, even if the connection is longer as complete.

A confession allows another person to see one's deepest flaws. An apology acknowledges those flaws to people who already know about them. A confession lays bare one's limitations; an apology places these limitations in another's hands to be accepted or rejected. Apologies are like secrets. A secret told increases the power of the listener and decreases the power of the teller, but either can do with the secret what he will.

An apology transfers power. A person who has withheld an apology has never given the listener a chance to reject him. A person who apologizes hands over the future of a relationship to another. (This is one reason that so many people refuse to apologize. They would rather harm someone and walk away than allow another the power to reject them.) The unspoken apology holds a petty kind of power. It prevents criticism, anger, or demands for promises. It protects against rejection. In the spirit of forgiving, though, which requires an unwavering commitment to truth, an apology is the only real means of opening up the potential of reconnecting with the person one has wounded.

Like the rest of forgiving oneself, humility is at the core of an apology.

THE POTENTIAL OF AN APOLOGY

An apology, once it has left a person's lips, can fall on unresponsive ears or be immediately responded to. The following is a schema of where an apology might go:

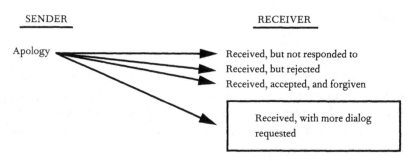

Dialog requested on the part of the listener is the response that a person attempting to forgive himself hopes for. (If his apology had been accepted earlier, he could have probably forgiven himself long before.) An apology received but not responded to places the future of the relationship in another's possession. That person may or may not respond at some later time.

If dialog opens up it may, and usually does, include requests for explanations, expression of feelings, condemnation, and demands for promises to be made so that the listener begins to feel safe again. The promises are for assurances that the listener will not again be betrayed.

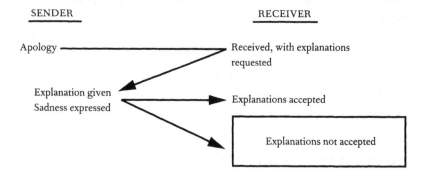

If explanations are not accepted, the relationship may be put on hold until the listener considers them carefully or the relationship may close at this point. If explanations are accepted, the dialog can continue. If the explanations are not accepted, the listener may want to express his feelings and anger.

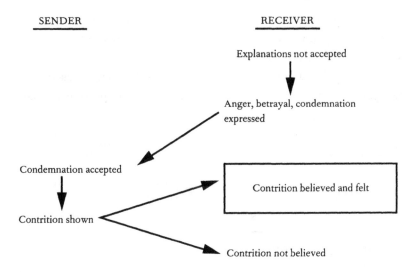

If the feelings behind an apology are not accepted, the person offering the apology can again attempt to convince the other of his honesty; but there is little more he can do.* Regardless of whether the exchange ends at any of these junctures, the person who harmed the other has made every effort to reconnect with the one he hurt. The reconnection, however, does not necessarily result in repair. If the listener accepts the apologizer's contrition, the dialog can continue further.

If promises are not accepted (or even if they are), there will likely be a long "trial period" during which the injured person can assess whether the other really follows through on his promises.

If the dialog initiated by an apology runs its full course, a breached or damaged relationship may be reaffirmed by both people and begin to move, however shakily, forward again.

Donald might decide to use the problem-solving strategy of apologizing to complete the process of forgiving himself. If he does, he will

---

*Domestic quarrels in abusive homes sometimes occur after one person thinks he has humbled himself by apologizing to another. When the apology is not accepted, the abuser can think of no way to take back his power except to abuse the other verbally or physically.

contact one of the men in his platoon and apologize to him. If the man listens politely, but wants no further dialog, Donald will have, at least, accomplished two objectives: He will have broken his silence and acknowledged to a person he betrayed that his behavior caused him to feel pain; and he will have given the other man an opportunity to communicate at some later time, should he choose.

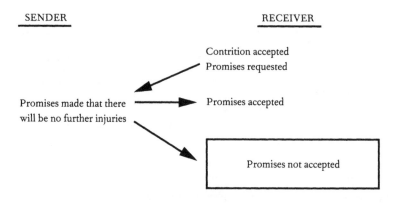

If the other soldier chooses to talk to Donald about his experience of abandonment, then the apology may result in the soldier's forgiving Donald immediately, or the soldier's requesting more from Donald. He may want more information. He might demand a written apology. He may condemn Donald for his lack of leadership and bravery. In other words, when an apology is delivered, there may be some negative repercussions at first; but usually a person who apologizes is well aware of that possibility and goes ahead anyway. Connecting with another person is worth the price.

Surrogate Apologies

What if there is no one alive to apologize to, or if the person one hurt is unwilling to talk? Is there anything a person can do?

Ordinarily an apology takes the form of this schema:

Person A apologizes to Person B.

When Person B is unavailable, he can sometimes be replaced with a "stand-in" or surrogate. Two schemata for "surrogate apologies" are these:

Person A apologizes to Person C (a surrogate) for hurting Person B

or

Person A apologizes to Person B (a surrogate) for hurting Person A.

Suellen (A) chose the first schema to put the final touches on forgiving herself.

⤞⤝

Suellen's son (B) had been troubled all his life. He became cocaine dependent and was involved in drug dealing. He was a chronic liar and a user. Suellen's friend, Barb (C), had watched the sorry drama of Suellen's life for years and knew that Suellen blamed herself because she had married an alcoholic whose problems absorbed much of Suellen's emotional resources at a time when her son was at a critical developmental stage.

Suellen has increased her self-esteem through years of therapy and has become reconciled to the fact that she and her son will never repair their relationship until he gives up drugs. She stopped blaming herself, to some degree, because of the influence of Al-Anon friends. Still, time after time in her daydreams, she wants to apologize to her son for letting him down. She believes if she could do this, she will finally forgive herself.

One day, Suellen (A) called Barb (C) and asked her to come talk with her. She told Barb she wanted her to role play as if she were her son (B). Barb agreed.

Suellen poured forth an apology. She told "her son" that she had not meant to hurt him and that she was very young and confused herself at the time he was a young boy. She asked "him" if he understood or might even contact her again.

Barb answered that she understood and that someday Suellen's son would also understand. Barb accepted the apology completely. Suellen felt enormous relief. If Barb, who knew her well, could accept her apology, maybe someday her son could too. Suellen felt connected with Barb and her son in a very new way.

Louise used the second schema to apologize to herself.

For a lifetime, Louise believed that she had hurt herself permanently for "allowing" herself to be sexually assaulted by her father. She knew, rationally, that she had been only a child, but could not convince herself that she was not to blame. Louise had explained her feelings to her therapist, who suggested she apologize to "herself."

People can apologize to pictures, tombstones, or even holes in the ground. Louise chose to apologize to her own picture placed on an empty chair. She told the picture she was sorry she had not been strong enough to fight her father off or brave enough to try to escape him. When she was done with her apology to herself, she turned to a second empty chair nearby and pretended she was her own grandmother, speaking to the young Louise in the empty chair. As her grandmother, who had loved her very much, she told "Louise" that there was nothing else she could have done. She was forgiven. Louise felt immediate relief.

☙❧

Apologies, whether directed to an injured person or to a surrogate, open communication. They can lead to cautious acceptance, angry silence, loving responses, or lengthy dialog. Whatever the result, a person who apologizes reaches out for human connection and, in giving up power, feels his humanity and humility even more than before.

Restitution

The second problem-solving method that a person can use to complete the process of self-forgiveness is restitution. Like an apology, making restitution reconnects an offender with humanity.

Restitution is an equivalent payback. If a child breaks a window with a stone, he makes restitution when he pays for a window of equal value. But how can a person make restitution for an injury that is so damaging it has remained unforgiven? In a real sense unforgiven injuries are in a category by themselves because no equal restitution can be made. How can a person give back a life or someone's self-esteem or trust? He cannot. In less severe losses, though, restitution might be a remaining possibility, either in actual form or again in "surrogate" form.

☙❧

Jocelyn was named her niece's godmother, a title that meant a great deal to her sister-in-law. It meant nothing, by contrast, to Jocelyn. Even after Jocelyn's brother died, when her niece was only two, Jocelyn never extended herself to the child. She never took any special notice of the girl's life; in fact, she never even sent greeting cards. For twenty years, Jocelyn told herself that the girl was distant and wanted no relationship with her. Then it dawned on her that she was ashamed and "guilty of neglect." Jocelyn is trying to make up for lost time. She is also confronting herself and putting her defenses aside.

"My niece is relatively unresponsive to me as a friend, relative, a young woman. . . . I'm beginning to see that her personality is not self-revealing [and that] I neglected her. [Now] she and her mother and I do travel to be with each other and enjoy [being together].

"This forgiveness thing can help me accept myself, instead of feeling less a person because I am not a nurturing, child-centered person."

Time is what Jocelyn can give her niece. Even if she cannot make up a lifetime of "lost moments," she can give a future of meaningful moments now that she has chosen to do so.

Donald, too, could make restitution in the form of time. He cannot pay back lost leadership or make up for battlefield wounds, but should he choose to continue the process of forgiving himself in a way that reconnects him with those he betrayed, he could give back some time to those from whom he had withheld it.

SYMBOLIC RESTITUTION

When people cannot pay for the harm they have done in kind, they do have other options, some of which are becoming regular newsmakers. People can, and do, make symbolic restitution for injuries they have caused. This kind of restitution also serves to humble people and help them connect again with the community.

Drunken drivers who kill may not be able to restore life, but they can reach back into the community by sharing their insight and warning others about the dangers of drinking and driving. Prisoners who are chronic criminals can give back to their communities by holding sessions with young first offenders to dispel any myths they may have about the romantic nature of criminal life and prison. A man who smoked until he got lung cancer, can speak out to schoolchildren about the dangers of smoking.

When there is no way a person can repay the one he hurt for the damage he has done, he can make symbolic restitution to the human community. Any community has opportunities for people waiting and wanting to make restitution. And total self-forgiveness, for many people, comes when this restitution is complete.

The coping strategies—social comparison, benefit analysis, and appraisal-, emotion-, or problem-focused strategies—all help to bring the stages of self-forgiveness to a finale. Confronting yourself (Phase 1) gives a person a glimpse of himself he has not been able to accept. Holding yourself responsible (Phase 2) helps a person identify himself as the one in need of forgiveness. Confessing your flaws (Phase 3) lets another person know that you are aware of your limitations or wrongdoings. Transforming (Phase 4) provides links back to the human community. For some people use of a coping strategy will allow them to forgive themselves, even though regret may linger. For others, still more profound transformation will be the final key to self-forgiveness.

Transformed Assumptions

Personal transformation takes its most complete form when a person goes beyond the ordinary coping strategies of dealing with life's stresses and, instead, fundamentally changes who he will be in the future and how he will see his world. This kind of transformation happens when a person's bedrock assumptions have been so destroyed in the wake of the unforgiven injury that he must rebuild them from the bottom up. In this kind of transformation, a person is forced to rethink the nature of human beings and how he fits into that nature. He also rethinks what the essence of the world is and how he can live his life meaningfully.

In Chapter 1, I said that there are six bedrock assumptions that form a person's "assumptive set." They are that one's self is worthy, that the world is benevolent, and that the world has meaning.[41] In addition, most people hold dearly to assumptions that justice exists and that they have some control over matters in their lives—that they are not mere pieces to be moved about on some gigantic game board.[42]

When people cannot forgive themselves, they have come to believe that they are not worthy—that they are some kind of "beast" in a "sea of angels." They think that they have little control over life's destiny; after all, they have lost what has meant the most to them—love, freedom, friendship. They struggle to believe that the world is benevolent or has any intrinsic meaning at all.

Writers, scholars, and theologians have struggled to capture the nature of the human persona. From the book of Job in the Bible to Shakespeare to Mark Twain to Stanley Kubrick, "man's" character has been the subject of poetry, movies, plays, treatises, and scripture. Most conclude that the human species is essentially terribly and tragically flawed, but that its individual members construct delusions that protect them from that knowledge. The species may be greedy, envious, murderous, petty, jealous, tyrannical, and incapable of telling truth; but the individual person deludes himself that he is, somehow, an anomaly of the species to which he belongs. He, by contrast, is loving, honest, altruistic, and without envy.

As individuals, our delusions, defenses, and denials usually cover up the truth of our natures. Most of us can watch the news and experience some degree of shock at the people around us (not ourselves) who do wicked things. If we are not shocked, we are inured to what "those people" do—what the "beasts among us" are capable of.

If some evidence of the human "dark side" emerges (for example, if a jealous person slashes his lover's car tires), individual defenses are called out immediately to protect us from the terrible fact that we each share this dark nature with all other human beings. Humans are graced with brains that can suppress, deny, rationalize, intellectualize, or just plain repress our vile sides. Ernest Becker, the Pulitzer Prize–winning cultural anthropologist, put it this way:

The defenses that form a person's character support a grand illusion, and when we grasp this we can understand the full drivenness of man. He is driven away from himself, from self-knowledge, self-reflection. He is driven toward things that support the lie of his character, his automatic equanimity. . . . We flirt with our own growth, but also dishonesty. . . . One must be born, not as a god, but as a man, or as a god-worm, or a god who shits. . . . Full humanness means full fear and trembling, at least some of his waking day. . . .[43]

People who cannot forgive themselves are those whose defenses have given way to reveal their true characters. They have come face-to-face with their own humanity. Their deluded assumptions about themselves no longer hold. These people will have to rebuild their bedrock assumptions about who they are: not angels and not beasts, but instead flawed humans in a flawed world.

Humans, if burdened with the disquietude of the truth about themselves do, however, have some advantage: When they drop delusions of uniqueness, they are free to join others who are like themselves.

Imagine going to a party. As you enter, you see angels on one side of the room. They are clustered together talking about their good deeds and lofty goals. On the other side of the room are the beasts. They are congratulating themselves for their treachery and complete lack of virtue. You, the beast-angel, know you are not so unique as a beast. You have evidence to the contrary: You have felt contrition and guilt for harm you have done. You also know you are not so unique as an angel. You have evidence to the contrary: You have done such damage that you must forgive yourself. Where do you go, then? With whom will you spend your evening?

In the corner of the room are, thankfully, all the other beast-angels. They are sharing stories of their good deeds and stories of struggling to overcome envy and greed. They are laughing at their own foibles.

It is to this group that people who are trying to forgive themselves belong. The beast-angels' delusions about themselves are gone; they are free to struggle to be the best they can be. But they know that they are no better, no worse, than any other human. To be a good human is a choice, not a character trait.

"Humility" is defined as "the state of being humble in spirit: freedom from pride or arrogance."[44] A person whose delusions have so fallen that he cannot protect himself from seeing his own wickedness can, through self-forgiveness, gain a wonderful, unexpected freedom. He can be free from the burden of pridefulness. His new assumption about himself as "flawed, but human" allows him to see the world as both malevolent and benevolent because it is made up of other people. These new assumptions pave the road back for the person seeking self-forgiveness to rejoin other humans who are just like himself. And, being so, they can forgive each other for their common frailty.

Mark Twain wrote:

> *Of all creatures that were made, he [man] is the most detest-*
> *able. Of the entire brood he is the only one—the solitary one*
> *that possesses malice. That is the basest of all instincts, pas-*
> *sions, vices. . . . He is the only creature that inflicts pain for*
> *sport, knowing it to be pain.*[45]

We are faced with the prospect of learning how to forgive everyone, including ourselves, or remaining unable to forgive anyone. Unless some of us are angels and some beasts, there is no other logical conclusion to draw. Being mere humans, we must forgive ourselves and go on, so that we can make whatever contributions we have time left to make.

Purification Rites

Apologies and restitution reconnect people with those they hurt and communities from which the wounded came. People's new assumptions about full and flawed humanness draw them together in a spirit of mutual forgiveness. Purification rituals, the third mechanism for reentry into the human endeavor, can reconnect people with each other and with spiritual entities, or both.

A Christian person who believes that his wrongdoing or meanness has severed him not only from the ones he hurt but also from God and other Christians, can seek purification through rites such as repentance, confession, or baptism. When he does this, he can go to heaven with others in the "family of God."[46] If God can forgive him, then he should also forgive himself so that the gift of life is lived in happiness.

Baptisms can reconnect Christians with the meaning of life, as can other purification rituals from other kinds of belief systems. Amrit, for example, is a ceremony in Sikhism that is very similar to Christian baptism. Blessed water is poured on a confessant to purify him. Yom Kippur, Judaism's most holy day, ritualizes repentance of all the previous year's sins. Zen Buddhists can reestablish their covenant with others in repentance ceremonies. The litany is hauntingly humble and can be said silently, or aloud to the offended person, or to no one in particular:

> *All evil actions committed by me since time immemorial stem-*
> *ming from greed, anger, and ignorance arising from body,*
> *spirit and mind, I now repent having committed.*[47]

Some purification ceremonies purge; others are symbolic of reconnecting with other people and the spiritual world. Ingesting or inhaling something one believes is magical is a ritual that rejoins people. An Apache song says:

> *It was a sad thing you did;*
> *It was a sad thing you did:*
> *But now we smoke together;*
> *The smoke will gather inside us.*[48]

Some groups of plains Indians, particularly the Crow and Sioux, believed that warring and friction displeased God so much that their relationship had to be frequently revitalized. To do this, plains Indians utilized, and utilize, sweat lodges in their purification ceremonies. The lodges symbolize the universe. People enter through a low door that represents the finite nature of man. The darkness inside symbolizes human ignorance.

When the ritual of cleansing and purging is complete, the people leave their ignorance inside to have it "forgiven and put behind."[49]

Other sects, ethnic groups, or even families have purification rituals that suggest forgiveness and recommitment. What is so important, where forgiving is concerned, is that each of these methods is a community purification ritual, and not one engaged in only by the individual and for one's own benefit.

A purification ritual that fosters forgiveness of oneself or anyone else must connect people to others. It is not enough just to be cleansed. In light of this, something must be said here about "new age" purification rituals.

"New age" purification rituals (for example, colon therapy, rebirthing, holotropic breathwork, Hakomi Mind Body Therapy, Chakra Balancing, and so on) are used to connect the individual person with his own neglected or forgotten spiritual aspects and his own body, but not necessarily any other person; and certainly not with his own humility.

Regarding Chakra Balancing:

> *A single purpose lies behind all of these methods of Chakra Balancing: to allow vital life energy to flow without restriction throughout the body, which helps the body in healing itself.*[50]

Regarding Hakomi Method of Mind Body Therapy:

> *The objective of the Hakomi Method is to facilitate personal growth and transformation. Through various processes, people are able to discover, study, and revise limiting beliefs about themselves.*[51]

About Rebirthing:

> *A Rebirth takes approximately one to two hours. . . . Rebirthers believe the process of conscious, connected breathing integrates*

> *body, mind, and spirit, and helps an individual maintain a*
> *perpetual state of health, happiness, and abundant energy. . . .*
> *Rebirthing is the principal mechanism for putting divine life*
> *energy back into the human body and mind.*[52]

Any of these rituals may be wonderful for self-healing and for gaining insight and reducing stress. None of these, however, has the dual purpose of community purification rituals. None cleanses and connects. The person who forgives himself must do both: He must feel clean and connected once again—to others, to God, or to both.

Exercises for Phase 4: Transformation

These exercises can be undertaken to complete the fourth phase of self-forgiveness. With self-forgiveness nearly complete, you may have a few remaining tasks you can use to finally complete the process.

Exercise 1: Gifts

People who forgive others and themselves are able to find gifts from their experiences.[53] These gifts may be lessons they have learned about themselves or lessons about life they never could have learned without suffering non-forgiveness.

1. In your journal, set aside a page or two for you to list the gifts you have received because of the unforgiven experience. These may be spiritual insights, people who have helped you, or help you have been able to give others.
2. Once a week reread your gift list and add to it when you can. Share the list with another person (a therapist or friend) if it seems appropriate to do so.

You may have confessed the harm you brought to others or yourself, but not apologized directly to the person you hurt. Apologies can be accepted or unaccepted. They can open doors; or doors will remain closed. Still, it may be important for you to give another person the power to accept or reject your statement of contrition.

Exercise 2: The Apology

Plan a way to tell the person you hurt or betrayed that you are sorry. If possible, apologize in person. (If not, select a close friend or someone who knows you well to listen to your apology.) You want to consider these important parts of an apology. It should:

1. State your wrongdoing clearly
2. Contain no excuses or justifications
3. Make it clear how badly you feel
4. Ask the person to whom you apologize to reconsider engaging in a dialog with you

If your apology is accepted, then you can reassure the listener that you will not betray him again. If it is not accepted, the listener may choose at some later day to talk with you. Either way, you profit.

Some people can find ways to make restitution for their mistakes. The next exercise is designed to help you consider how you could pay someone back for your wrongdoing.

Exercise 3: Paying Back

Consider these two questions:

1. Is there any way you can pay for the harm you did? (For example, if you took money, can you return money? If you took time, can you return time?)
2. Who is the person you believe you should make payments to? If you have identified the person and the method, think about a strategy for making the payback. For example, if you could pay back money, determine a repayment schedule of some sort that you can realistically afford. If you could pay back time, etc., what is realistic in terms of how you might accomplish this?

3. Next, write or call the person you want to pay back and make your offer; or send a representative. If the offer is accepted, put it in the form of a written promise and begin immediately to meet your obligation.

Exercise 4: Symbolic Paying Back

If there is no way to make up for the harm you have done, find a symbolic way to make payments to your community. (For example, if you hit someone while you were driving drunk, find a way to make speeches in your community about driving responsibly and responsible drinking. If you let down your elderly parent by not giving him enough of your time, volunteer your time at a nursing home.)

Once you have decided the best way to make restitution, set your plan in motion. Start immediately.

Your assumptions about yourself and the world around you have dramatically changed once you have damaged yourself, another, or a relationship beyond repair. If you forgive yourself, though, you have rebuilt these assumptions.

Exercise 5: Assumptions

Most journal entries include extensive notes about your feelings about other people. In this final exercise, write your views about yourself. Whom would you compare yourself to, for example? What will you be doing in a few years? What would your best contribution to life be?

Summary

If you have completely forgiven yourself, you have thrown off self-hatred and exchanged it for accepted regret. Your regret is the regret of thinking and feeling humans who know that we are all flawed and, unless we are lucky indeed, we leave hurt behind us as well as the legacies of our good deeds.

When you have forgiven yourself, you can feel the sweet relief of receiving and accepting an invitation to come back into the human community.

I asked the people I interviewed and those who completed questionnaires what they would tell readers about self-forgiveness. This is what some of them said:

> *"Ego or arrogance is the primary cause of individual suffering and pain. Discharging one's ego and reaccepting oneself as human, frail and with faults, is the beginning of understanding the purpose of our existence."*

> *"Self-forgiveness is essential for self-love and the ability to love and understand and forgive others. . . . [I feel] acceptable, gentle, comfortable, and humble. (No more need to self-justify or defend.)"*

> *"I feel clean, renewed, energized. Additional feelings for my husband."*

> *"Self-forgiveness is such an effective emotional weight reduction program—so freeing. It changes your perception of life."*

> *"It is a long process. Be gentle with yourself. People have remarkable strength, courage, and resiliency. . . . [The key experience to it was] finally designating fault."*

> *"Imagine someone or something you would feel compassion for if you found them hurting inside, be it a loved one, an animal, a stranger, or even a plant. Imagine how you would feel if you found them, how much you would want to help them feel better before you even knew what's wrong. That is the Christ in you reaching out. Now place yourself as that someone. Feel Christ reaching out to you. You deserve compassion. You deserve forgiveness. You are loved."*

"I feel free, accepting . . . sorting out blame [was most important]."

"To carry old baggage through life is just a way of giving your power away. It makes you stand still in the growing process. I feel positive to finally have put it to rest. Feels like a new freedom of one's self."

"Self-forgiveness is necessary for physical and emotional comfort. The stress and physical and mental work required are worth it. I made a mistake and I learned from it."

"I feel whole, okay with all the sadness and hurt; I'm free to live [and] less fearful of death. Take the risk."

"I did the best I could with the knowledge I had. The first marriage could have been saved with the knowledge I have today, but I didn't have those skills/tools fourteen years ago. When I was born, I was not guaranteed that people . . . would treat me fairly. I am responsible for my own happiness, growth, fulfillment. Because I have failed at having good marriages does not make me a bad person."

"Be gentle and loving with yourself. Learn the lessons. For it is with those lessons that we become whole, contributing human beings. . . ."

"I feel relieved! No matter how hard it is we must forgive ourselves. If we believe we did the best we could, we must forgive ourselves, and ask for God's guidance and go on. Otherwise, your health and well-being will be affected by your feelings."

"Many times people hold on to punishment being the only way to be forgiven. I have found that my maturation through the holy spirit is the secret to forgiveness. If Christ forgives me as

I clumsily plod through my life, then why shouldn't I forgive myself?"

"If we allow our shame to exist, it will control us. And it will never be in a positive way. Forgiveness opens us to the positives of life. It brings us from the darkness of shame to the joy of living."

"I feel much more free to not be carrying that burden anymore. We are often our own worst enemy by being such harsh judges. No one is perfect!"

"I feel a stronger sense of self-esteem and more humble. Making amends/restitution is always an imperfect art. We put forth our best effort and choose to grow in our sense of self, others, and God. . . . Forgiveness is a gift of grace that is bigger than ourselves."

"An important thing for me to get rid of the nagging guilt feelings was first of all to admit I failed—instead of making excuses for myself. Then I could have something tangible to handle and could say—Yes, I failed."

"Whatever you think you did to someone else, you were doing to yourself. What was it? How can you treat yourself better? Do it."

"I would stress the fact the no parent, no teacher, no adult should ever teach children about a God who will condemn them to hell if they do something wrong. . . . I finally can say it was all a lie, and I am free."

PART III

The Limits of Forgiveness

THE people in Part II were able, with hard work, to forgive themselves and free themselves from self-hatred. To many readers, their accomplishments are probably considered to be positive. The struggle of self-forgiveness forces those who harm others to commit themselves to a process of self-reflection and personal change. Because of this, people who have forgiven themselves can be seen as assets to their friends, communities, and society because they are unlikely to repeat their mistakes.

But should there be limits to forgiveness? Are there people who do not "deserve" to forgive themselves? Part III addresses this question and suggests some answers.

CHAPTER 9

The Limits of Forgiveness

"I know about your work, and I think you are dangerous and irresponsible," growled the angry voice of the caller. I was being interviewed on Wisconsin Public Radio on a beautiful summer day in 1992. The host and I were discussing my first book, *Forgiving the Unforgivable,* and the people I had met as I was writing the book who had managed to forgive some horrible injuries. That caller was the first I encountered who harbored extreme and negative feelings about forgiveness: but he would not be the last. The caller went on to say that if people forgive each other, they release people from their responsibilities. He believed forgiveness gave wrongdoers *carte blanche* to go out and hurt people again.

I explained that I thought he was confusing pardoning with forgiving. When an authority pardons a wrongdoer, the wrongdoer is free to go and free of debt. When a person forgives another, by contrast, it is one of life's most intimate and profound experiences. Forgiveness takes work; pardoning is conferred. The forgiver frees herself of hatred, but does not free the injurer of responsibility, whether she forgives another or herself.

Soon after the radio broadcast, I sat on a panel of a TV talk show with a mother who had forgiven the drunk driver who killed her son. I watched, almost aghast, as the studio audience vilified the woman. A studio audience member stood up, pointed her finger, and called the unsuspecting woman a bad mother—irresponsible for forgiving the man. I tried to remind the audience that the man was paying off his debt to society: He was in prison. The woman tried to explain that she needed to rid her heart of her anger, and that the man had made a terrible mistake, but one many of us could make. After the taping of the show, the woman told me she had hoped to show people that forgiveness was possible; after this experience, though, she said she would never again subject herself to such cruelty.

People want blood. They want justice. But there will never be enough justice in the world to mend all the world's broken hearts. A little, or a lot of mercy, though, might just save us from drowning in hatred.

What is it about us that wants, even seeks and provokes, hatred? Why would an idea like forgiveness or self-forgiveness evoke the anger and suspicion that I have encountered over the years as I talk about the topic?

This final chapter of *Forgiving Yourself* is a treatise, or really a group of small essays, on forgiveness—particularly on how forgiveness could be resented or even hated. Among them might be enough particles of truth to provide some answers to the caller's anger—or our collective need to hang on to anger—to not allow forgiveness.

Beyond Forgiveness?

Jeffrey Dahmer, the cannibalistic murderer of young men (who was later himself murdered), sought God's forgiveness. He had written from his Wisconsin prison cell to a minister of the Church of Christ, Ray Radcliffe, who subsequently befriended him. Over time, the two men began to know each other and Dahmer asked to be baptized. The

Reverend Radcliffe, convinced that the murderer was honest in his quest to repent and gain salvation through God's grace, found a small whirlpool in the prison's infirmary and there performed the baptismal ritual. When it was complete, Mr. Radcliffe said that it had been a wonderful thing to see and that Dahmer thanked him. "There was a sense of joy and gladness in his heart. . . ."[54]

Susan Smith, the South Carolina mother who murdered her two young sons by rolling a car with them strapped into it into a lake, also requested and received baptism in prison. The minister who performed that ritual declared, "She sought forgiveness from the church and the Lord, and she knows it has been granted."[55]

Jeffrey Dahmer and Susan Smith were shut away from society to protect "us" from "them." Many more people, though, are like the individuals in this book than they are like Dahmer and Smith. Most people who hurt others are not evil, but they also have been shut away. They are locked in figurative prison cells where they remain hostage to their own guilt, shame, and remorse. The key question—for those of us who hurt each other but who do not actually sit in prisons—becomes: Who has the authority to release us? Must God forgive us? Must injured people forgive their injurers? Should injurers be encouraged to release themselves? A larger question may be this: Do most people really believe in forgiveness these days, either forgiving others or forgiving themselves? Or is forgiveness a concept that once made sense in less complicated times before we knew so much about incest, white-collar rip-offs, drunk drivers who kill, doctors who harm patients, and unfaithful spouses, among others? It may have been easier to talk in more uncomplicated times about forgiveness or to value forgiveness as a central practice of a civilized society.

Forgiveness has traditionally been considered a process in which an injured person releases his injurer from indebtedness and hatred. A forgiver, some think, has empathy for the one who hurt him and, through his understanding, invites the injurer back into the human community. "Forgiveness," wrote Hannah Arendt, "is the only real form of mutual release we have for each other. . . ." It incorporates a "constant willingness to change [our] minds. . . ."[56] Many people believe that one must seek forgiveness from another and then be freed from captivity by that person. This idea of forgiveness lies at the heart of Judeo-Christian thought. A sinner can repent, seek God's forgiveness, and have his sins washed away by God's grace. Also in the Judeo-Christian tradition, forgiveness "must be mobilized by men toward each other before they can hope to be forgiven by God also."[57]

If these beliefs are basic to our country's major religious schools of thought, should we not see forgiveness all around us? Would we not expect our politicians to tout the benefits of forgiveness? Should we not anticipate messages of forgiveness from pulpits? If forgiveness were valued, wouldn't Sally Jessy, Oprah, and Phil use stories of forgiveness to build their ratings and garner the support of sponsors? It seems that many people in our country are confused about forgiveness, retribution, and retaliation. From all appearances in the media, we are heading toward more mean-spiritedness, both interpersonally and politically, where forgiveness plays no role. Surely retaliation and revenge are safer than misplaced forgiveness. A forgiven person, after all, might spell danger to his family or community whether the forgiveness is conferred by another or by himself; and people might distrust self-forgiveness as much as they distrust the idea of an injured person forgiving the one who hurt him.

What are the arguments against self-forgiveness? How could we not endorse it as positive and proper?

Arguments Against Self-Forgiveness

The first argument one hears against self-forgiveness is this: Only an injured person is in the position to forgive someone who hurt him. He, alone, can open a door and invite the offender back in; and this invitation is extended only after the offender has done a number of things. First an offender must apologize. He must accept condemnation and acknowledge his wrongness. An offender must pay back his debts and promise the one he hurt that nothing hurtful will happen again.

In other words, forgiveness comes with certain punishments and price tags. It can be granted, the standard argument goes, only by a person who has been directly harmed. If an injured person chooses not to forgive his harmer, there must be a good reason. Perhaps he recognizes the injurer's potential to do harm, maybe worse harm than he has done already. If an offender forgave himself, this potential evil would go unrecognized. The checks placed on him by non-forgiveness would be removed and he would harm again.

The argument goes on, then, that if an injurer, in the absence of being forgiven by the one he hurts, forgives himself, he puts the rest of the human community in jeopardy. A person who forgives himself but has not been forgiven by another has not learned a lesson. He has not been punished, so he may not really understand how wrong or dangerous he is. Forgiveness is an exchange, a gift given by one person to another. No one can or should give this gift to himself. He cannot know how the other felt and cannot perceive and, rightfully, fear himself as others might wisely do.

As Part II, which describes the process of self-forgiveness, demonstrates, self-forgiveness is anything but letting oneself off the hook. Self-forgiveness takes hard work, honesty, humility, and real personal transformation. Thus, the argument that a person who forgives himself has not learned a lesson and may be prone to injure others again does not bear weight. The idea, also, that forgiving is and should be an exchange between two people may appear quaint. Even if we think people who forgive themselves make the rest of us unsafe, we may have to also acknowledge that in this day of rapid-fire relationships, physical mobility, moral turpitude, or just plain indifference where each other's feelings are concerned, forgiveness is quite likely to come from no one other than the self. So many people are unwilling to forgive their enemies or offenders, that often, no one other than the offender can forgive.

It does not take much more than a glance around your social network to see how many people do not believe in forgiveness. And although the argument that a person may not forgive himself until another has forgiven him may have some merit, in these times, it is often only the offender who is willing to do the hard work of forgiveness because the injured person is unwilling to engage in such a difficult process.

A third argument against self-forgiveness is that people who hurt others should live with their guilt and shame. The question for us then becomes, "For how long?" Must someone who lied or cheated or was unfaithful to a partner live in self-loathing for the rest of his life? That is, should he live a psychological life sentence? Even thieves and murderers are not expected to do this. At some point in time, they are set free. But a non-forgiven person faces a life sentence of remaining shut out of the human community. Do we really want this? Why would people in a civilized society want others to carry the burdens of self-hate and guilt around for a lifetime? Jeffrey Dahmer, Susan Smith, Charles Manson, and others who are simply evil perhaps should hate themselves for a longer period than those of us who merely harm our relationships. However, if we look more closely, those of us who harm our relationships also do indelible damage to other people even if we do not take their lives. If we want certain people to hate themselves, who decides who these people are? If all of us should hate ourselves, what happens to us as a human community?

A fourth important question is this: Why would a person who did something terrible want to go through the struggle of finding forgiveness? Should he not have to live in shame and the guilt that accompanies wrongdoings and limitations? If a person forgives himself, he frees himself from perpetual self-loathing. What value to society does a person who doubts his worth and places little value on himself have? Self-forgiveness, examined in the light of these questions, can be viewed as a positive goal for us all. For someone to play his full role in society, he cannot be burdened by self-loathing and self-hatred. These emotions require too much energy to maintain, and each is, in a real way, self-indulgent. If a person hates himself, he ruminates on his guilt; his energies stay focused inward rather than being available to his fellow citizens. In light of this, some would consider forgiveness a moral duty, because where there is non-forgiveness, hatred is allowed to spill over onto other people. If forgiveness is viewed as a duty, then it is the duty to restore peace where hatred has been. Therefore, in the absence of being forgiven by another, one could argue that it is a duty to forgive ourselves, no matter how much work and self-examination it takes. If it is a moral duty to stop hatred, then when a person refuses to forgive himself, he allows hatred to go unchecked; and hatred in any form is destructive to our society.

The outcome of forgiveness—either forgiving another person or forgiving ourselves—is that peace is restored to the human community. When people forgive others, they stop the hatred and thus prevent it from spreading. When people forgive themselves, they step back into the community, reassume their responsibilities, and teach others how to refrain from making the same mistakes.

What is the human community in America today? A better question yet: Is there a community in the United States, or are there so many different "communities" that forgiveness between people from other groups is impossible?

Verna, a woman who was badly beaten, considered herself a key member of the "battered women's community." She set up the local battered women's shelter in her town. Five years after her divorce, she decided to forgive her ex-husband. She chose to do this because, she believed, her lingering hatred for him was making her sick. Verna simply wanted to live more happily. Her decision, however, was met with outrage when Verna told others in the "women's community" that she had had a nice dinner with her "ex" during which she forgave him. She said she felt wonderful and free. The two had parted, as they began their relationship many years before, with a kiss on the cheek.

When word got out, Verna's "friends" were furious. They told her that forgiving her ex-husband sent a loud and dangerous message to the men in their area that battered women were tolerant of batterers. Verna explained that her forgiveness was extremely personal and not a political statement of any kind. Not accepting her explanation, the shelter board fired her.

᠅᠅

Ian, a young Caucasian driver, ran over an African-American boy who ran out in front of his car from between two parked cars. Ian could not have missed the boy. He immediately sought out the parents to apologize and offer to help pay the boy's hospital bills. The parents accepted his apology. Ian began to forgive himself.

When word reached the African-American community that the parents had accepted Ian's apology and money, the community was outraged. They issued a press statement that streets in the African-American community were too narrow and that traffic was purposely diverted onto them by city officials to increase the possibility of young black men being killed. Under pressure, the boy's parents issued their own statement about Ian. He was a white oppressor, they said. They would not accept "white man's guilt money." Ian once again found himself in the throes of hatred—especially the hatred of others.

᠅᠅

The Politics of Forgiveness

In Verna and Ian's situations, one of the most intimate choices a person can make, to forgive oneself or another person, was so deplored by members of their "communities" that they were criticized for it. Individual apologies and acts of compassion were conceptualized as betrayals of one's larger reference group. The intensely personal became political. Personal forgiveness that had reached across the chasms between individuals was construed as negative bridge-building between two enemy groups.

Over roughly thirty years since the fragmentation of the civil rights movement, oppressed people in the United States have pulled farther and farther away from the central identity that, at least in appearance, once held us together. People who once identified themselves as first and foremost American citizens began to think of themselves as belonging only to small groups of fellow citizens. Oppressed people have increasingly united around smaller nuclei of people and called themselves "communities."

The various "rights" efforts (civil rights, women's rights, senior rights, gay rights, and so on) have become movements that coalesce into "communities," each of which has generated its own leadership, financial base, information network, lobbying organizations, and mission statements. Today, there are the women's community, the gay community, the environmental community, the Hispanic community, the African-American community, the educational community, and the university community, among others. The quick shift in allegiances and identity from heterogeneous communities, such as local, state, or national communities, to homogeneous communities of similarly-minded people, might be one of this country's most subtle, yet profound, changes.

Wars are going on in America, not declared civil wars, but wars on paper, among fund-raisers, and between neighbors who live next door to each other, but identify with vastly different networks of like-minded people. Neighbors, although side by side, may reside in different communities.

The oppressed have made many strides. There are many more people of color and many more women holding public office, for example. Relative to white men, white women make more money than they did thirty years ago. In some states, gay people can teach or work for the government without fear of formal reprisal. The visible and strident have made progress (the poor, less vocal, have not). But what is this progress toward?

Some might argue that when justice became that which American people sought most from our society, public discourse about how we are to be citizens of our communities shifted from what we owe to our communities to what we expect from our society. Thus, the discussion of "rights" has dominated public discourse for more than thirty years. Gone are discussions of our duties to each other. The Harvard law professor Charles Fried put it this way:

A positive right is a claim to something—a share of material goods, or some particular good like the attentions of a lawyer or a doctor . . . while a negative right is a right that something not be done to one. . . . Positive rights are inevitably asserted to scarce goods . . . negative rights [are] the right not to be interfered with in forbidden ways. . . .[58]

Modern communities, each with their own agendas and beliefs that they are deprived of their rights, try to lay claim to their portion of resources. Money, advancement, and educational opportunities, for example, are rights they believe must not be interfered with. Unfortunately, one community's agenda may interfere with another community's ability to attain its goals.

Forgiveness between individuals who are members of vastly different "communities" might be construed as flirting with the enemy. If the personal is political, then to restore peace between individuals will require peace treaties or formal resolutions, not forgiveness. If forgiveness and self-forgiveness are feared or vilified, how can people cleanse their hearts and minds of hatred and make peace with other people?

The past thirty years or so may, indeed, have resulted in strides for the oppressed; but if forgiveness has succumbed to political pressure, what is left for hurt and angry people except isolation? We need bridges across the chasms that separate us: If forgiveness cannot be that bridge, what can we put in its place?

What has our society done with forgiveness? What has become of this most intimate form of peacemaking? What is our society teaching children about forgiveness, one of the few forms of peacemaking we can actually influence? Especially important is what "baby boomers" in our society are teaching their children about forgiveness. This generation, especially, has altered the complexion of the country—interpersonally, politically, economically. In this community, divorce is commonplace, affiliation with churches and religious groups is down, and the incongruity between those who see themselves as lovers of peace and those who see themselves as staunch supporters of the "republic" is greater than ever. Self-forgiveness, if it is to be valued, must be taught as a method of restoring peace. For baby boomers, peace may be equated with world peace, but there is very little an individual can do about world peace. World peace starts with peace among family and friends.

Forgiveness begins at home with our ex-spouses, estranged children, resented parents, and discarded friends. Peace can be granted. Peace can also be earned.

But peace does not come easily. It is a struggle and it takes work. The one source of peace available to anyone, man or woman, young or old, black, white, yellow, or red, is forgiveness. There can be no quarrel that forgiveness restores peace, and how can peace in any form be as dangerous as revenge and retribution?

The Nature of the Beast

Maybe it is the "nature of the beast" to resist forgiveness. Maybe it goes against some aspect of human nature. Some thinkers postulate that righting wrongs between people who have hurt each other is almost a human need;[59] but others have penned adages that must, at least a little, reflect human nature:

> "It is human nature to hate those whom you have injured."
> —Tacitus
> "The offender never pardons."
> —George Herbert
> "When they have injured, they also hate."
> —Seneca

Listening to someone talk about forgiveness or watching it in action, an observer might frame forgiveness as too moral, too good to be true—too idealistic. Many of us love idealism, but only if it stops short of seeming to be outright hubris.

In a sense, forgiveness, perhaps more than most endeavors we engage in, brings out our essential nature, our strange dualism. Dualism here means that humans have two competing desires: the desire to be special, to stand out from others; and the desire to be a part of something much bigger than ourselves.

Ernest Becker called the tension between our need to be unique and our desperation to merge with some larger meaning or force the "absolute tension of dualism."

> *You can see that man wants the impossible: He wants to lose his isolation and keep it at the same time. He can't stand the sense of separateness, and yet he can't allow the complete suffocating of his vitality. He wants to expand by merging with the powerful beyond that transcends him, yet he wants while merging with it to remain individual and aloof, working out his own private and smaller-scale self-expansion. . . . One obviously can't have merger in the power of another thing and the development of one's own personal power at the same time. . . .* [60]

When people forgive others and themselves, they leave the company of angry, alienated people and merge with something that is within our capacity to have, but which most of us are unable to achieve: the merger of love and compassion in the face of hatred. When people forgive, they transcend the rest of us who are stuck in our small hatreds. In this way, they increase their own personal power. Forgiveness unites the dual nature of our beings by embodying, in one act, transcending and merging at the same time.

The bitter family member who watches a wounded loved one forgive her injurer can feel helpless when the forgiver walks away from hatred and leaves it and the family member, figuratively at least, behind. When we watch other people forgive themselves, we sense their merger with something big and beyond us; and then it is we who feel shut out and betrayed.

No one wants to be abandoned, even if it is by our own anger or poison that we have been left behind. The accomplishment of forgiveness can provoke jealousy and anger in the face of the fact that some of us can, and do, transcend our pettiness and flaws.

When people forgive themselves for hurting others in their lives, they leave the rest of us behind. They reconcile their humanness and transcend it at the same time. Forgivers have found the way to peace, while the rest of us watch in confusion, anger, or envy.

What is it that we want for ourselves and each other? Do we want people to live lives of ceaseless guilt? Do we want drunk drivers, incest perpetrators, adulterers, liars, and cheats to spend entire lifetimes lost in self-conscious self-denigration? Do we want mercy to take a different proportion to justice in our society, acknowledging that today, justice seems to be most people's primary concern?

Forgiveness and self-forgiveness require that a person take a brave stance toward some condition in his life that cannot be changed. As Viktor Frankl put it:

> *Whenever one is confronted with an inescapable, unavoidable situation, whenever one has to face a fate that cannot be changed . . . just then is one given a last chance to actualize the highest value. . . . For what matters above all is the attitude we take toward suffering, the attitude in which we take our suffering upon ourselves.*[61]
>
> *In a word, each [person] is questioned by life; if he can only answer to life by answering for his own life; to life he can only respond by being responsible.*[62]

The essence of human existence lies in the stance any person takes toward a fate he cannot change. We, individually and collectively, need to grapple together to determine what stance we want each other and ourselves to take when we have been hurt by or hurt others. Retaliation and revenge are one option. Forgiveness of ourselves and others is another. Whichever we choose, each of us must respond to life by being responsible. In times when peace seems rarely at hand, forgiveness and the peace it brings may be the most responsible choice that we, independently or as a people, can make. Forgiving yourself for the mistakes you have made is a small step toward peace. It is a signal to others that you have learned from, and are again engaged in, the activities of life.

Notes

INTRODUCTION

1. E. Kurtz, "Not God." (A one-day workshop on The Intellectual Significance of Alcoholics Anonymous, University of Wisconsin-Whitewater, April 8, 1982.)

2. J. Landman, *Regret* (New York: Oxford University Press, 1993), 104.

3. *American College Dictionary*, 1964, s.v. "mistake."

4. Landman, 104.

5. *Webster's New International Dictionary*, 3d ed., s.v. "shortcoming."

6. Ibid., s.v. "limitation."

7. R. Janoff-Bulman, *Shattered Assumptions* (New York: The Free Press, 1992), 5.

8. B. Flanigan, *Forgiving the Unforgivable* (New York: Macmillan, 1992), 73–90.

9. Ibid.

10. Ibid., 7.

11. Janoff-Bulman, 11–12.

12. See, for example:

D. Crenshaw, *Bereavement: Counseling the Grieving Throughout the Life Cycle* (New York: Continuum, 1990).

G. Kaufman, *Shame* (Cambridge: Schenkman, 1980).

J. Landman, *Regret.*

C. S. Lewis, *A Grief Observed* (Toronto: Bantam Books, 1964).

M. S. Strobe, W. Strobe, R. O. Hanson, eds., *Handbook of Bereavement: Theory, Research, and Intervention* (Cambridge, England: Cambridge University Press, 1993).

13. See, for example:

W. G. Justice, *Guilt and Forgiveness* (Grand Rapids: Baker Books, 1980).

H. Morris, *On Guilt and Innocence* (Berkeley: University of California Press, 1976).

P. Tournier, *Guilt and Grace* (San Francisco: Harper and Row, 1958).

14. W. Gaylin, *Feelings* (New York: Ballantine, 1979).

H. Morris, *On Guilt and Innocence*, 59–63.

J. Landman, *Regret*, 36–56.

15. E. Kurtz, "Why A. A. Works," *Journal of Studies on Alcohol*, vol. 43, no. 1 (1982), 67–72.

16. Morris, 60–61.

17. Landman, 47.

18. Crenshaw, *Bereavement.*

C. S. Lewis, *A Grief Observed.*

CHAPTER 3

19. J. A. Martin, "A Realistic Theory of Forgiveness," in *The Return to Reason*, ed. J. Wild (Chicago: Henry Regnery, 1953), 315.

20. Janoff-Bulman, 123–130.

CHAPTER 5

21. Janoff-Bulman, 6.

22. Janoff-Bulman, 125.

CHAPTER 6

23. H. S. Kushner, *When Bad Things Happen to Good People* (New York: Schocken Books, 1981).

24. *Sex Roles*, vol. 8, no. 4 (April 1982).

25. See interviews throughout in Flanigan, *Forgiving the Unforgivable.*

CHAPTER 7

26. *Webster's Third*, s.v. "admit."

27. S. Bok, *Secrets* (New York: Pantheon, 1982), 76.

28. Ibid., 79.

29. Ibid., 76–83.

30. Ibid., 76.

31. Ibid., 82.

32. Ibid., 75.

33. Ibid., 76.

CHAPTER 8

34. Flanigan, 162–163.

35. Janoff-Bulman, *Shattered Assumptions*; R. H. Moos and A. G. Billings, "Conceptualizing and Measuring Coping Sources and Processes," in L. Goldberger and S. Breznitz, *Handbook of Stress* (New York: Free Press, 1982), 218–219.

36. Janoff-Bulman, 117–120.

37. V. Frankl, *Psychotherapy and Existentialism* (New York: Simon and Schuster, 1967), 14–18.

38. V. Frankl, *Man's Search for Meaning* (New York: Washington Square Press, 1963).

39. Landman, 212.

40. Moos and Billings, 218.

41. Janoff-Bulman, 6.

42. E. Becker, *The Denial of Death* (New York: Free Press, 1973), 47–66.

43. Ibid., 56.

44. *Webster's Third*, s.v. "humility."

45. M. Twain, *The Autobiography of Mark Twain* (New York: Harper, 1959), 122.

46. R. Radcliff quoted in E. Brixley, "Can a Murderer Go to Heaven?" *The Wisconsin State Journal*, Madison, Wisconsin, July 10, 1994, 6G.

47. The litany was recited by Jean Schneller of the Zen Center, Madison, Wisconsin, during a telephone interview, July 28, 1994.

48. G. Cronyn, ed. *American Indian Poetry* (New York: Ballantine Books, 1962), 357.

49. T. E. Mails, *The Mystic Warriors of the Plains* (Garden City: Doubleday, 1972), 152.

50. M. Kastner and H. Burroughs, *Alternative Healing* (La Mesa, California: Halcyon, 1993), 151.

51. Ibid., 101.

52. Ibid., 209.

53. Flanigan, *Forgiving the Unforgivable.*

CHAPTER 9

54. E. Brixley, "Can a Murderer Go to Heaven?" *The Wisconsin State Journal*, Madison, Wisconsin, July 10, 1994, 6G.

55. J. J. Holland, "Killer Mom Says God's Forgiven Her, She's Ready to Die." *The Capital Times*, July 10, 1995, 1A.

56. H. Arendt, *The Human Condition* (Chicago: University of Chicago Press, 1958), 240.

57. Ibid., 239.

58. C. Fried, *Right and Wrong* (Cambridge: Harvard University Press, 1978), 110.

59. Becker, 150–155.

60. Ibid., 155.

61. Frankl, *Man's Search*, 178.

62. Ibid., 172.

Appendix

ATTRIBUTION THEORY

I. H. Frieze. *Women and Sex Roles: A Social Psychological Perspective* (New York: Norton, 1978).

S. Graham, V. Folkes, eds. *Attribution Theory: Applications to Achievement, Mental Health and Interpersonal Conflict* (Hillsdale, NH: Lawrence Erlbaum Associates, 1990).

J. Jaspars, F. Fincham, M. Hewstone, eds. *Attribution Theory and Research: Conceptual Development and Social Dimensions* (New York: Academic Press, 1983).

C. Peterson, S. F. Maier, M. E. P. Seligman. *Learned Helplessness: A Theory for the Age of Personal Control* (New York: Oxford University Press, 1993).

M. E. P. Seligman. *Learned Optimism* (New York: Knopf, 1991).

Sex Roles, vol. 78, no. 4, April 1982.

K. Shaver. *The Attribution of Blame: Causality, Responsibility, and Blameworthiness* (New York: Springer-Verlag, 1985).

K. Shaver. *An Introduction to Attribution Processes* (Cambridge, MA: Winthrop, 1975).

S. Zelen, ed. *Attribution-Personality Theory Conference, 1988: New Models, New Extension of Attribution Theory* (New York: Springer-Verlag, 1991).

Index